KADYBEAUTY SEER

The Alchemy of Hair and Healing

Transforming lives through Hairdressing and Reiki Healing

Khadijatou Ndoye

Copyright sNotice

DEDICATION

To my Royal Family

Kings, Queens, and Crowned Children of Light

This work is lovingly dedicated to you my extended soul family, who have graced my sacred chair over the years. Each of you has brought more than just hair to be touched. You brought your stories, your prayers, your hopes, your fatigue, your joy, and your desire to be seen, felt, and honored. And in return, you allowed me to pour into you. So this legacy is not mine alone. It is ours.

with unwavering love and reverence Kadybeauty

"Kadybeauty Seer"

Holistic Hairdresser | Sword of Truth | Healer of Crowns In the
salon, she holds space for kings, queens, and crowned children of
light. As an author, she weaves stories of truth, self-worth, and
divine remembrance. Her words, like her hands, awaken the soul.
Kadybeauty Seer is not just a name it's a mission. This book is her
offering to the world A testimony. A ritual. A return. With every
braid, every parting, every loc, she channels prayer, power, and
purpose.

TABLE OF CONTENTS

Prologue

Khadijatou, known as Kadybeauty, is a holistic hairdresser, Reiki Master healer, artist, poet and spiritual guide whose salon is more than a beauty destination, it's a sacred space for transformations. Born in Senegal and spiritually awakened through her life journey across Africa, Europe, and the U.S., she has fused ancestral hair rituals with modern healing practices. As a seer and intuitive, Kady weaves energy work, Ruqyah, and deep intention into every braid, twist and cut, helping clients reconnect with their inner divinity. Her signature styles reflect more than beauty; they radiate purpose, faith, and truth. Through her work and writing, she invites readers to embrace self-love, spiritual alignment, and divine identity.

Her signature styles reflect more than beauty; they radiate **purpose, faith, and truth.** Through her work and writing, she invites readers to embrace **self-love, spiritual alignment, and divine identity.**

"And We send down of the Qur'an that which is healing and mercy for the believers…"

(Surah Al-Isra, 17:82)

This verse embodies her calling — to be a vessel of mercy, healing, and light through the sacred craft of beauty and energy.

The Whisper Before the Crown

By Kadybeauty Seer

Before the braid,
before the blade,
before the oil touched root
or the prayer met scalp

there was a whisper.

A whisper from the womb of stars,
from the ancestors who braided the cosmos

and wrapped destinies in golden thread.

They called me not just to style

but to see.
To anoint every strand with sacred intent.
To cleanse with water.
To cut with truth.
To crown with love.

My chair is more than a seat.
It is an altar.
A confession booth.
A mirror to your becoming.

This book is not just pages
it is a ritual,

a remembering,

a return.

Come.
Let your hair down.
Let your soul rise.

You are not here by accident,

you were called,

same as I was.

This is the beginning

of your healing.

Introduction

Hello Dear Lovely Royal Family !

Welcome to a journey of beauty, spirit, and transformation inside out ! This book is not just about hairdressing and Reiki healing, but is about tapping into a wellspring of energetic shifts that can turn your life around in a positive way, My name is Khadijatou but my clients called me Kady, I'm thrilled to share my world with you, a realm where hair isn't just hair, but healing that goes beyond mere touch. I want to take you back to the moment I realized my passion wasn't just about styling but how much is about connection, craft, love, passion , integrity, dedication, consistency, patience, Faith, trust, honesty, compassion, commitment and community. It all started in my early age , shaped by cultural, religious, spiritual influences and a deep-seated calling. The beauty industry, to me, was always more than skin-deep; it became a sacred Divine vessel for healing and transformation.

As you dive into the chapters of this book, you'll explore my experiences and learn the techniques that have not only redefined the way I see hair, but also how I perceive healing energy through Reiki (energetic life force) spiritually and Ruqyah (religious healing true the Holy Qur'an) It relies solely on the Qur'an and authentic adhkār (remembrances) taught by Prophet Muḥammad ﷺ (PBUH) Peace be Upon Him no incantations, magic, or non-Islamic rituals are involved. To seek Allah's protection and cure for illness (physical, emotional, or spiritual), alleviate distress, and ward off harm.

Each section is designed to peel back the layers of my journey and showcase the artistry that goes into every strand of hair and every healing session I conduct. I invite you to discover my go to styles and tools that ignite a spark of creativity, presenting hair as a living canvas that reflects inner beauty.

Reiki is interwoven into my narrative, forming a beautiful dance of my own hands with the scissors and brushes I brandish . Throughout our time together, I'll guide you through Reiki's foundations and illustrate how this ancient art complements my hairdressing practices. You'll gain insights into the sacred rituals I perform, creating an environment where my clients can not only look good but also feel rejuvenated and uplifted.

Speaking of clients, their stories are the beating heart of my journey. Get ready to hear profound true testimonials, these are powerful, turning points that showcase the black girl magic that happens when we align art with healing. Each transformation will remind you just how interconnected our lives are. Their stories echo the same themes of energy, alignment, and the importance of community, resonating with each of us as we traverse our personal paths and journey.

But wait, there's more! We will delve into how to align your energies, creating an irresistible magnetism in your own life. Transformation, after all, is not just about the external; but a holistic approach of feeding the spirit while styling the hair. This book will empower you to embrace self-care practices that bring balance and harmony to your life, illuminating the profound impact of community on personal growth.

Every page invites you to participate actively in this journey. You won't just be an observer; you'll be a part of an alchemical process that allows for deep emotional and spiritual nourishment . As you read, I encourage you to reflect on your own experiences and be inspired to cultivate your own unique healing practices.

I can't promise this will be an easy ride; the journey of self-discovery often comes with bumps and turns like a bad hair day! Yet, I assure you, it's also immensely rewarding. I'm excited for you to explore these lessons and blessings from my chair and the connections forged behind the salon mirror with the permission of my Lord (Allah SWT) [الله سبحانه وتعالى (Allāhu subḥānahu wa taʿālā), which means "God (Allah) is glorified and exalted"] By the time you reach the end of this book, I fervently hope to inspire you to take your hair and healing practices to soaring heights.

So grab your toolsets and be it scissors or crystals and Holly Books! Let's embark on this transformative adventure together. Remember, healing begins from within, and beauty is just the cherry on top. Always be grateful to go within so you don't ever go without your Inner G. (God Guidance). Remember you're the reflection of your Lord the Most High and you're destined for greatness, and I'm absolutely honored to be your guide along the way!

With all my heart, love and light and abundant healing energies !

Kadybeauty Seer the Holistic Hairdresser and the Sword of Truth

Embracing Healing

Khadijatou, known to her clients and friends as Kadybeauty, had always found solace and joy in hairdressing. The rhythmic snip of scissors and the gentle caress of a brush gliding through strands and chakra alignment had a transformational power that delighted her deeply, it's like wielding a sword of truth. Little did she know, however, that her journey was about to widen, inviting her to explore the unseen dimensions of healing beyond the external beauty she crafted with her hands.

It began one evening after closing time, as Kadybeauty sat alone in her softly lit studio. The steady hum of the salon's neon sign outside mingled with the faint scent of lavender and rosemary from her homemade hair elixirs. She closed her eyes and placed her hands gently on a client's shoulders, feeling more than hair and scalp beneath her fingertips as she sensed a subtle resistance, a shadow of anxiety tucked behind tense muscles.

That night, Kadybeauty dreamt of a vast, moonlit desert where a cloaked figure offered her a slender, ornate dagger. "This is your sword of truth," the figure (ancestors or spirits guide) whispered, "but its edge cuts deeper than mere appearances." When she awoke, her first thought wasn't of haircuts at all, but of the quiet yearning in her client's posture.

Over the next weeks, she began to weave simple rituals into her appointments: a whispered blessing before the first snip, a guiding breath exercise as she applied nourishing oils, and a brief moment of silence at the end of allowing each person to integrate the cut and the calm. Word spread: clients emerged not only looking radiant, but feeling unburdened, as though a hidden weight had been lifted.

Intrigued by this gentle alchemy, Kadybeauty dove into the study of energy work and sound healing. She learned to listen for discordant vibrations in the aura, to trace the root of physical tension back to emotional knots, and to dissolve them with the vibration of her voice or the soft chime of a singing bowl. Each time she aligned a client's chakras, it was as if she carved away a layer of illusion and revealed the authentic glow beneath.

One afternoon, an older woman arrived, her shoulders stooped under the weight of grief. As Kadybeauty combed through her silvery hair, she felt a heavy thrum of sorrow. Remembering the desert dagger from her dream, she closed her eyes and let her hands rest over the woman's heart, softly intoning the verse, "Verily, with hardship comes ease" (Q. 94:6). The client's breath softened and tears slid down her cheeks; when the session ended, she thanked Kadybeauty, calling her a "swordbearer of the soul."

In that moment, Kadybeauty understood her true path: not merely to style hair, but to wield her gift like a sword of truth and cutting through the illusions that keep people from their own light, and guiding them back to wholeness. And so, with every snip and every healing tone, she stepped further into the unseen realms, confident that beauty without depth was only half the story.

One crisp autumn afternoon, as the leaves danced on the wind outside her bustling salon, Kady received an unexpected invitation from a friend, a renowned Reiki master named Amina. This invitation sparked curiosity but also a thread of skepticism in Kady's heart. After a long week of styling, the thought of attending a healing workshop felt both intriguing and vaguely intimidating. The concept of energy healing was still relatively new for Kady, someone who had always focused on the tangible aspects of beauty: the shine of healthy hair, the sculpt of a perfect cut, sophisticated braiding style and the exuberant joy on a client's face after a transformative style. She couldn't help but think, how could touch mere , touch can promote anything more than the aesthetic?

Nonetheless, her dream was a compass and the allure of stepping into a new realm prompted her to accept the invitation. When the day came, Kady's excitement waned slightly as she arrived at Amina's cozy studio, filled with soothing aromas of lavender and sandalwood. The walls whispered tales of serenity, adorned with crystals that caught the sunlight, refracting it in vibrant colors that danced in the air. A sense of calm washed over her as she entered, yet apprehension bubbled inside her, a little hesitancy about what lay ahead.

Amina greeted Kady warmly, her peaceful aura instantly comforting. As they settled into a circle of chairs arranged on the soft, bamboo floor, Kady felt a gentle pull towards Amina, who exuded an air of wisdom she couldn't quite define. Yet there still lingered that bit of skepticism that made her question if this energy work was merely a placebo, a mirage crafted in the minds of those seeking solace in an increasingly chaotic world.

As the workshop began, Amina introduced the principles of Reiki's origins. My friends, Reiki is an art and science of energy healing that requires less training than how you pronounce , the flow of universal energy, and how it connects us all. She explained that Reiki isn't about the healer but about channeling energy to facilitate healing. Kady listened intently, her initial doubts softening in the warmth of the atmosphere and the sincerity in Amina's voice. A part of her recognized the truth in the interconnectedness that Amina spoke of, especially in her own craft as a hairdresser. The careful, nurturing touch(is about channeling the energy through her anointed hands) she extended to her clients wasn't just a physical act; it embodied a connection, an exchange of energy that ebbed and flowed between her and those who sat in her salon chair.

As the workshop continued, Kady participated in a hands-on exercise where participants paired up for a practice session. Her partner, a gentle soul named Fatima, laid down on a yoga mat, radiating trust. Kady placed her hands just above Fatima's body, hesitating initially, unsure of what she was supposed to feel. Was there really energy flowing? Was this all just a figment of positive thinking? But as she closed her eyes, drawing her breath deeper, she allowed herself to be enveloped by the tranquility around her.

In that moment, the world dimmed behind her eyelids, and she began to sense a tingling sensation, subtle yet captivating. It was like the air itself had become a delicate current of warmth, dancing just beneath her palms. Kady's intuition stirred, and she felt compelled to let go of her skepticism. With every breath, she focused on channeling love and healing to Fatima, her hands guided by an instinct she hadn't recognized before.

"A little higher on the right side," Amina instructed gently, guiding Kady's hands. With each minor adjustment, Kady perceived the vibrant energy shifting; it was a language of its own, one that released what Fatima had been holding onto. When the session ended, Fatima slowly opened her eyes, tears glistening on her lashes. The gratitude she expressed echoed with a resonance that jolted Kady's heart. At that moment, something fundamental sparked within her soul and a newfound understanding that healing transcended appearance; it embedded deeply into the fabric of being.

During the debriefing that followed, Kady found herself sharing her experience, her voice trembling with emotion. "I felt something I never thought I would. It… it was unlike any connection I've experienced while working with hair," she admitted, her vulnerability seeping openly into the sacred space they had created together. The others nodded in acknowledgment, their eyes lit with similar revelations.

As days turned into weeks, Kady continued to reflect on the experience, her apprehension fading. That initial introduction to Reiki became a lantern lighting her path toward integrating healing into her hairdressing practice. She began to experiment with infusing energy work into her sessions, observing how her clients reacted when she focused on alignment and intention while styling. Each appointment became a dance of exploration; every cut of hair, braids or twists for locs, or even taking down braids, every application of dye transformed into a ritual that encompassed both aesthetic creation and energetic exchange.

However, Kady also faced an internal conflict that stemmed from the duality of her paths. The world of hairdressing and the world of energy healing had been so distinct in her mind. Could she truly merge both as one? How could she maintain her identity as a skilled hairdresser while embracing this new aspect of healing? Each session at the salon felt like a tug-of-war of sorts,(dark night of the soul) where she grappled with the fear of navigating uncharted waters while attempting to hold space for her clients as a healer.

Her initial trepidation manifested during one unexpected appointment. A client named Selma from Waco , she sat in her chair, a brilliant and ambitious woman who had recently experienced a significant personal loss. As Kady began to style Selma's hair, she sensed an heaviness that permeated the air around them as a medium, a weight that went beyond mere sadness, a burden residing deep within her client's spirit. It felt almost palpable, and Kady's instinct as a healer urged her to reach out.

With careful deliberation, she started to engage Selma in conversation, allowing the energy of trust and vulnerability to intertwine between them. "You can talk to me about anything you are feeling," Kady said softly, feeling the warmth of her hands still through each fiber of hair on her scalp as a channel for positive energy "Sometimes expressing those thoughts helps to lift the weight."

Selma hesitated, her eyes flickering. Then, with a soft sigh, she began to share her heart touching story about the loss of a beloved family member, the overwhelming grief, and the struggle to find joy in what remained. Kady felt her heart swell with empathy as she listened. It wasn't just about the hairstyle; this was a moment of healing. She allowed herself to engage with Selma on a level that transcended the artistry of hairdressing.

"I want to offer you something special today," Kady proposed gently. "If you're open to it, I could incorporate a bit of energy healing while I work." Selma looked surprised but intrigued, and after a pause, she nodded.

As Kady styled Selma's hair, she also placed her hands softly on Selma's shoulders, her fingers delicate yet firm. She began to channel the energy that she had felt that day in Amina's workshop. With every stroke of her hands, she visualized healing energy flowing from her palms, working its way into Selma's being, unraveling the knots of grief she felt within.

A serene silence enveloped them; the usual chatter in the salon faded as Kady focused on her intentions. She bypassed her own uncertainty, diving into the innate trust she felt in the transformative power of connection. Selma's breath eased, and Kady felt the heaviness begin to dissipate, replaced by a wave of warmth flowing through them both.

When the appointment concluded, Kady turned Selma toward the mirror. The fresh style reflected not just an external transformation but an internal one as well; Selma's eyes shone anew, a reminder of resilience. "You truly have a gift, Kady. It's more than just hair," Selma said, her smile revealing the profound impact the experience had created.

The beauty of that moment filled Kady with warmth, affirming her intuition that hairdressing and healing were not only complementary; they were intertwined, each enhancing the other. In recognizing this, she began to embrace both identities, learning that she had the power to facilitate healing through touch while amplifying her artistry through intention.

As Kady continued to grow in her practice, she invested time in her education about Reiki, exploring various techniques and philosophies. She began to weave them deeper into her hairdressing sessions. During appointments, she would create an ambiance of healing soft melodies voiced Qur'an playing, scents of essential healing oils embracing the air, and an atmosphere rich with positive affirmations spoken softly as she worked. Each detail contributed to an environment where healing could flourish.

In her salon, Kady not only crafted hairstyles but also initiated a safe space where her clients could open up, express their truths, and engage in the healing they may not even realize they needed. Whether it was a simple trim or a complex color treatment, the underlying intention remained steadfast: that beauty should not only reflect the exterior but also nurture the soul.

Kady quickly recognized that embracing healing had shifted not just her work; it also transformed her way of seeing the world. No longer were clients mere clients. They became fellow travelers in a journey of growth receptacles of stories, experiences, and wisdom. The energy exchanged was a tapestry woven from mutual trust and vulnerability; it empowered both Kady and her clients to navigate their own paths of healing and self-discovery.

Eventually, Kady began to bubble with excitement as her dual journey expanded beyond the confines of her salon. Thriving on the impact she had witnessed in her clients, she envisioned workshops that would integrate both hairdressing and Reiki, creating space for collective healing within her community.

With every step she took, the journey felt less like a burden and more like a calling, an invitation to weave her artistry with the threads of healing energy she had come to embody. She found everything came full circle; the gentle touches that had brought transformations within the realm of hair would spark spiritual awakenings beyond it, making Kady's path as a hairdresser and healer a sacred journey of empowerment, beauty, and authentic connection.

In taking this leap toward embracing healing, Kady had unlocked the door to self-discovery, a path filled with boundless possibilities. It was more than just a journey about hair or healing; it was a voyage of the heart, one she was now ready to embark upon fully, shining brighter than ever before while bringing her clients along on this incredible adventure. She stood poised at the precipice of what her work could become, ready to harness the power of energy and artistry to craft not just hairstyles, but meaningful experiences that would ripple through the lives of everyone who entered her world.

The Awakening of Kady beauty

Kady's Early Influences

Khadijatou , as the world would come to know her as Kadybeauty , was born into a tapestry of unshakable faith in Allah (swt) traditions and cultural richness. Growing up in the vibrant community from Ouakam of Dakar, Senegal, in West Africa , was surrounded by the echoes of laughter, the rhythmic beat of djembe drums of the rhythms of her tribe Lebous (Ndoye), and the warm, comforting aromas wafting through her grandmother's home Ndoyène Ripp. It was here, amidst these sensory experiences, that Kady's early influences began to take root, nurturing her passion for beauty and self-care.

Her Aunt Thiaba, was a matriarch in every sense of the word, not only a guardian of Kady's family history but also a master hairdresser revered within their neighborhood. Kady often found herself entranced as she watched Thiaba work, her hands deftly moving through the coils and curls of her clients' hair at a lightning speed , transforming their looks and, in turn, their spirits. The ritual began with an offering of small bowls filled with fragrant oils of coconut, shea butter, jojoba, amla and argan, all lovingly prepared and infused with herbs picked from their garden. Each scent told a story, each blend carried the essence of generations past in all lifetimes.

Kady recalled the sun filtering through the open windows of their modest home, illuminating the tiny particles of dust dancing in the air as her Aunt Thiaba carefully heated the oil. The subtle sizzle seemed to echo the murmurs of Kady's own excitement, as she anticipated the tremendous transformation that would ensue, both in terms of looks and the joy it would bring. Tata Thiaba would often hum traditional songs, their lyrics filled with wisdom and love, creating a sacred space that transcended the physical act of grooming. It was as if the act of hairstyling was a form of alchemy, blending the tangible with the spiritual quest.

"Every woman is a queen," Thiaba would often say, her voice warm and reassuring. "To care for their hair is to honor their crown chakra ." This phrase echoed through Kady's mind, each syllable embedding itself deep in her psyche, shaping the way she viewed beauty. The practice of hairdressing in her community was not merely about aesthetics; it was an essential ritual of respect, empowerment, and identity. Kady started to connect her love for hair to these broader ideas, realizing that beauty was an intricate part of the cultural fabric that enveloped her, it was her birthright.

During her first early years , Kady was often found perched on the edge of her Tata's chair, mesmerized by the way she effortlessly intertwined braids or tucked away stray ends with precision and care. It was during these lessons that Kady learned the importance of intention, each stroke of the comb, each twist of the braid infused with love. Absorbing Tata Thiaba's teachings not only provided her with technical skills but also a sense of purpose and connection to her ancestry.

As Kady grew, she began to experiment with her skills, offering to style her friends' hair during special gatherings. The pride she felt when her friends would twirl in front of the mirror, beaming with joy at their transformed appearances, ignited something within her, a flickering flame of passion that begged to be explored further. She cherished those moments, fully aware that the joy transcended the physical; it was a communal expression of beauty that deepened their bonds and created shared memories. Each laughter filled session curled into Kady's heart, further solidifying her desire to become a catalyst for positive transformation, a beacon of light.

Yet, as with any journey of self-discovery, there were moments of doubt. The adolescent years brought with them a whirlwind of change, and Kady found herself grappling with her self-identity in the face of societal expectations. She learned that beauty standards, especially in a world intertwined with Western ideals, could sometimes be harsh and unyielding. Her skin, a rich shade of mahogany, and her textured hair often felt scrutinized in environments that lauded straightened hair and lighter complexions.

Kady remembers the day she went to her first school dance 08/17/1988 at Stella Maris(elementary school) when she was only 9 years old, nervously anticipating the moment when she would reveal her outfit to her classmates. She had spent hours styling her own hair into an intricate pattern of braids adorned with colorful beads. When her friends complimented her, their words were like an embrace, wrapping around her insecurities and lifting them away. But, as the evening wore on, Kady overheard whispers" bad gossip " comments about her hair, her body shape , and the way she carried herself. A wave of self-doubt crashed over her, forcing her to question the very thing she once celebrated.

It was during these turbulent times that Kady turned back to her Aunt's wisdom. In those moments of uncertainty, Thiaba would remind her that hair could be a language, a way to express one's identity, but it could also be a tool of strength. "Hair tells our stories, Kady," she would say. "Embrace yours, no matter the noise around you." These words resonated deeply within Kady, initially soothing her wounds and later empowering her to embrace her authenticity.

As the years progressed, Kady developed a more nuanced understanding of beauty that aligned with her upbringing. She began to appreciate the fluidity of cultures, recognizing that beauty was not a singular representation. In doing so, she completed a cycle, returning to the empowering notion that she could reframe her narrative. The art of hairstyling was once a simple outlet for creativity but became an avenue for education, awareness, and healing within her community. She traveled to Milan, Italy in May 2001, got married for the first time in December 2004 in Torino, Italy and she was blessed with her son Mouhamed she called him her angel 1111 (a reminder of a stable home) because he was born in November 11th a near death experience at his birth that triggered her first awakening and her daughter Mina Bella is her angel 123 (one step at the time and to believe in divine timing) was born in January 23rd. After dreams and premonitions, as a chosen One born Seer, knew that God was not done with her yet! She heard in the spirit realm "Kill, Effortlessly, Evil, Narrative "(Killeen) that urges her to be obedient and the wonder of conquering the world and being more than a hairdresser she ended up in the United States of America in May 2012 in Killeen , Texas.

This awakening did not solely rest on her shoulders; it echoed throughout her community. Kady's friends, inspired by her confidence and newfound perspective, began to embrace their own hair journeys. Together, they explored styles that celebrated their roots, coordinating elaborate braids and vibrant adornments that honored their heritage. The salon became a safe space where laughter filled the air, and not just hair was transformed; healthier hearts opened, and connections strengthened.

In this environment of Killeen Texas , Kady embarked on her journey towards becoming Kadybeauty. Her hands began to work not just with the intention of crafting hairstyles but also as vessels of healing. It became clear to her that beauty was not confined to the surface; but ran deeper, intertwined with the essence of who people were. She harnessed the lessons of her childhood, blending the relatively mundane act of hairdressing with the profound act of energy exchange she would later learn through Reiki healing.

Kady's early influences were not merely stories of brushes and creams; they were tales of resilience, identity, and the heartwarming strength found within her community. The physical beauty she learned to respect was birthed from a deeper understanding that had been passed down through generations, reminding her and those around, that nurturing one's appearance is a journey, interwoven with the threads of heritage, culture, and love.

As she prepared to step into the world beyond her grandmother, parents , the village and Aunt's embrace, a sense of determination enveloped her. She sought to carry forth the legacy of her heritage, to weave the ancient traditions of beauty into the fabric of modern practice. Her understanding of hairdressing blossomed as it aligned with her heart's calling. No longer would hair merely be viewed as an accessory; it would be revered as a crown, an expression of identity, and a clear channel for divine connection.

Through Kady's lens, beauty transformed into a powerful medium, guiding the way for her clients to discover their own inner strength through a journey that she had first embarked upon in her aunt's salon at the tender age of five and continued to celebrate as she found her voice within the world of hairdressing and healing in Killeen. The ritualistic practice of hair and self-care became a sacred exchange, far beyond the superficial, as Kady became the embodiment of her aunt's teachings but a visionary who would soon bring KadyBeauty (inner & outer beauty) into the lives of many, reminding them that they, too, were inherently worthy of honoring their beauty.

Defining moments

As I stepped into the salon for my very first day of work, the air was thick with the scent of hair products and shampoos, conditioners, and a hint of hair spray that clung to the walls like an unspoken promise of transformation. The bustling noise of clattering scissors and lively chatter echoed around me, a symphony of excitement and anxiety that resonated deep in my chest. I had dreamt of this moment for years, yet now, as I stood at the threshold, nerves tangled like the strands of hair I would soon sculpt into something beautiful, the intoxicating mix of fear and anticipation paralyzed me. What if I failed? What if I wasn't enough?

It was a cozy neighborhood salon that felt more like a home than a workplace, adorned with vibrant artwork and mirrors reflecting bright personalities and lively interactions. I could see the stylists in action, each one lost in their own rhythm, expertly wielding their tools, gossiping as they transformed tired faces into glowing ones. I felt a flutter of envy coupled with awe; they made it look so easy.

"Can I help you?" a friendly voice pulled me from my reverie. I turned to see a woman with bright red hair and an infectious smile standing before me. Her name tag read "Carina," and she exuded warmth that instantly put me slightly at ease.

"I'm Kady," I stammered, extending my hand with a nervous smile. "Today's my first day."

"Welcome to the family! Here we hug! Don't worry; you'll find your groove." Carina's smile widened, and her confidence was a breath of fresh air. She gestured for me to follow her, and I stepped further into the salon, my sense of anticipation bubbling under the surface.

As the day progressed, I watched the seasoned stylists engage with their clients, exchanging not just haircuts, braids, locs, Senegalese twists and weaves extensions but snippets of their lives and their highs, lows, and everything in between. I absorbed the atmosphere, hoping it would help ground me in my own impending tasks. I had spent hours practicing, perfecting my techniques, yet even with all my preparation, I could feel the weight of unpredictability pressing down. What if I failed to connect? What if my hands betrayed me?

By lunchtime, my palms were slick with sweat as I practiced cutting and braiding hair on a mannequin, cringing at my uneven lines. But I had little time to wallow in self-doubt. I was called to assist Carina with a client, and the vibrancy of the moment rushed back with renewed intensity.

"Okay, Kady, let's show her how it's done," Carina said, gesturing towards the chair where a middle aged woman sat, glancing nervously at herself in the mirror.

The woman introduced herself as Amara , her voice a soothing melody that contrasted sharply with the trembling of her hands. "I hope you don't mind… this is my first time doing something different with my hair. I've been stuck in the same style for years," she said, her eyes flickering with a mix of apprehension and hope.

I could see the reflection of uncertainty in her gaze, a shadow that I understood all too well. "Change can be intimidating," I replied, feeling a sense of connection. "But it can also be freeing from what no longer serves your highest purpose . You deserve to feel beautiful."

Amara smiled shyly, and I could sense the flicker of excitement beneath her fear. With Carina guiding me, we discussed styles and colors while Amara shared some of her life experiences, her long battle with self-doubt and how she felt invisible within her own skin. Each word resonated deeply with me, highlighting not only her journey but mirroring my own insecurities that had shaped my path towards hairstyling.

I watched Carina work the scissors skillfully, every snip a declaration of intent; she sculpted Amara's features, framing her face and coaxing out the beauty that lay hidden beneath layers of self-doubt. The transformation was not merely aesthetic; the excitement was palpable, and I felt an irresistible pull to be a part of that black girl magic, to weave my energy into someone else's renewal like magic.

After several inches of hair fell, Amara's breath hitched when she saw the change in the mirror. "Oh my gosh, I love it!" she exclaimed, her eyes wide with joy as glimmers of newfound confidence danced across her face.

I loved the way the room lit up around her. The laughter, the commotion and everything exploded in a vibrant burst of energy. In that moment, something within me flickered alive, and the fear I had felt earlier began to wash away.

With Carina's guidance, I stepped in to add the finishing touches, my hands steady, working with intention as I brushed Amara's hair into soft waves. The connection I felt while doing this was profound. I poured my heart into gently curling her hair, using deliberate movements as though each strand wove itself not only into a style but also into the very essence of empowerment.

"Now, let's add some shine," I said, applying a light oil to her hair. It gleamed like liquid gold under the salon lights.

"Wow, I really feel beautiful," Amara said softly. I saw how her shoulders relaxed, her posture transformed. There was something refreshing in her tone, an undertone of reclaiming her identity through her choice of hairstyle.

And with that statement, I understood. This was it. The epiphany was to awaken what I wanted to do in my life, not just craft beautiful hairstyles, but also empower others to embrace their beauty and their stories. I yearned to be a sanctuary where clients could come not just to change their appearance, but to also embody the strength they often overlooked.

As Amara got up from the chair, I felt my heart swell with pride and joy. "Thank you so much, Kady," she said, her voice warm with gratitude. "You don't realize how much this means to me."

"Thank you for trusting me," I replied, the words escaping my lips with a sincerity I had not anticipated feeling at all. In that moment of epiphany, I recognized how hairdressing was not just about the hair; it was about connection but also about sharing a space where healing could happen, where beauty could be liberated from inside out.

With Amara's radiant smile ingrained in my memory, the rest of the day was a blur of colors, scissors, and laughter. Each client brought new stories, and with each appointment, I felt more rooted in my purpose. Still, the memory of Amara lingered, acting as a guidepost for my emerging path. Do you know the real reason why hair is so powerful? It's because of key minerals found in hair called silica, which is one of the main compositions of quartz crystal, sourced water from the Pitt, from fruit and nuts (I call it the Divine Blueprint) ! It acts as an antenna that is able to transmit and receive frequencies to the spiritual realm.

Weeks turned into months; I honed my skills under Carina's mentorship, refining my techniques while nurturing the emotional connections that formed in the chair. My confidence blossomed, rooted in each successful transformation, whether physical or emotional. I recognized that when clients stepped into my chair, they did so carrying their stories in their joys, their struggles, their unspoken fears. My role was to honor that narrative, helping them uncover the beauty within themselves that had long been obscured.

As I became more adept at hairdressing, the experience with Amara remained a touchstone for me, reinforcing my belief that beauty extended far beyond appearance. My passion for hairdressing began to entwine seamlessly with my interest in Reiki healing, both channels of energy flow and connection, each empowering the individuals who came to me.

As Kadybeauty there were days when I doubted whether I was capable or days when criticism hit harder than expected. Some clients were dissatisfied, and others arrived only to leave unchanged. Those moments stung and shook me, each one haunting me as I feared I had failed to cultivate the same healing experience Amara had found. In those times, I would close my eyes and recapture the spirit of that first encounter, reminding myself of the transformation I had witnessed.

As my skills grew, so did my understanding of the profound nature of self-worth and how intertwined it was with the artistry of hairdressing. My job was more than a profession; it was sacred work, a ritual of nurturing both the outer beauty and inner resilience of my clients. I embraced my role, eager to explore the healing potential that resided within me, urging me to connect and uplift others.

Reflecting on that significant moment with Amara, I understood that my journey was not just about mastering the craft of hairdressing but it was about embracing vulnerability and connection and how they intertwined with healing. I learned that change was transformative and contagious, and as I shared that energy with my clients, their transformations would ripple outward, affecting not only their lives but the lives of those around them.

I had become a conduit of empowerment, and with each snip of the scissors, braided styles, micro life locs, bomb twist, Kady's signature micro Nubian twist, Senegalese twist or Kady's bellessa locs, I joyfully surrendered to the journey unfolding before me. In that realization, a powerful defining moment solidified my commitment to the path I had chosen. Hairdressing was my alchemy, a sacred art through which I could inspire, heal, and celebrate the beauty in every individual that sat in my chair.

As I reflect on my journey thus far, I understand that, like the vibrant strands of hair I work with, my determination is a constant evolution in a blend of passion and purpose, skill and heart. And as I continue along this winding road, I remain dedicated to the transformative power of this craft for myself and for all those who trust me to touch their lives.

The Art of Hairdressing

Tools of the Trade

As I step into my salon, I feel a rush of exhilaration every time. This space, defined by its gentle hum of activity and the rich aromas of essential oils wafting through the air, is not just a workplace but my sanctuary. Here, I find solace and inspiration, surrounded by the tools of my trade that are extensions of my creativity and practice. Each tool holds a story, a memory, and an energy that enhances the artistry of my craft. Today, I want to introduce you to my favorite hairdressing tools, sharing their significance and the intimate role they play in my journey as Kadybeauty, the alchemist of hair and healing.

Let's start with the scissors. To many, they might seem like just an everyday item, but to a hairdresser like me, they are sacred instruments, the sharp blades that transform strands of hair into masterpieces. My pair, a vintage set passed down from my grandmother to Tata Thiaba then me, is particularly dear to me. Their Japanese steel glistens under the light, and their edges are keen enough to cut through the thickest of hair yet delicate enough for the finest snips.

My hands have grown accustomed to their weight and balance, which empower me to execute precision cuts. Each snip is intentional, a meditative motion that syncs with my breath. I remember the first client I used them on after receiving them, a young girl nervous about her first haircut. The moment the scissors made contact with her hair, I felt a wave of energy pass between us, and it was as if the air buzzed with anticipation. With each intentional cut, I not only reshaped her hair; I shaped her self-esteem. The scissors reflected my care and intention, acting as a bridge between her external transformation and her internal journey.

Next, I want to highlight my trusty combs. Like the scissors, they come in various shapes and sizes, tailored for different styles and textures. My favorites are the fine-toothed comb for precision, the wide-toothed comb for detangling, and the tail comb that serves both for sectioning hair and adding detail to styles. Each comb invites connection, creating a seamless interaction between my artistry and the hair I style.

One memorable instance comes to mind when I worked with a client who had long, flowing locks, tangled not just in hair but in life's challenges. I began by using the wide toothed comb, a gentle tool for easing her tension and stress. As I carefully worked through her hair, I felt the layers of her worries unraveling in tandem with the tangles. It was a healing experience for both of us, as my hands danced through her hair like a soft breeze, guiding her towards tranquility. The combs in my hands became conduits of energy, signaling our shared journey towards renewal.

Bringing color into hair is another area where my tools shine quite literally. My array of brushes and applicators is essential in creating vibrant hues that breathe life into my clients' styles. Each brush serves a purpose: the paddle brush for distributing color evenly, the round brush for adding volume during blowouts, and the precision brush for intricate color work.

I vividly recall a client who walked in wanting a bold transformation, a vivid red that spoke of confidence and passion. As I dipped my precision brush into the deep scarlet hue, I felt a wave of excitement and responsibility wash over me. Each stroke on her hair was an intention; I visualized the energy of courage and self-love flooding through her strands. As the color set, her eyes gleamed, reflecting the brightness she wished to embody. The brushes, much like my Reiki practice, became extensions of my energy, channeling the transformations we envisioned together.

Of course, no discussion about hairdressing tools would be complete without mentioning the hairdryer. This essential gadget serves not merely to dry hair but to sculpt and shape. I use my dryer to create waves and curls, infusing movement that dances in the light. One day, I had a client who was preparing for an important event but was feeling quite anxious about her hair. I used my diffuser attachment, allowing the warmth of air to caress her strands, as I encouraged her with gentle affirmations. What emerged was not just a hairstyle; it became a beautiful emblem of her strength, with each curl forming not just in her hair but in her heart.

Every great craftsman knows about maintaining their tools. My workspace reflects this philosophy. The organization of my salon is not mere aesthetic; it is a spiritual practice. Each tool is placed with intention, positioned in a way that creates harmony and flow. I keep my scissors, combs, brushes, and dryers within arm's reach, inviting spontaneity and creativity while allowing for a conscious choice at every moment. A small wooden tray by my station holds various oils and crystals, aesthetically pleasing yet thematically profound, encapsulating energy and intention. Each element radiates positive vibrations, as we prepare for the healing experience ahead.

As customers enter my salon, they are often welcomed by an array of inspiring quotes adorning the walls, each handpicked to resonate with the journey of transformation. "Your beauty is a reflection of your spirit," hangs prominently near the mirror, a reminder that every haircut , twist or braid is so much more than what meets the eye. This mantra resonates deeply with my work, encouraging clients to acknowledge their inner strength while I help shape their outer appearance.

Additionally, I have a corner dedicated to personal mementos: photographs from past events, thank-you cards from clients, my first page spotlight in Bell county magazine "she does it all" and images that stir my creativity fill the space with warmth. Each item is infused with memories of challenges overcome, smiles shared, and healing witnessed. This corner of my salon, rich in stories and energy, serves as a reminder of the community I serve and the interconnectedness of our sacred journeys.

As I stand behind my station, scissors in one hand and a brush in the other, I draw parallels between hairdressing and Reiki. Both involve meticulous attention and intention, an understanding that energy flows through us and into the world around us. Each time I pick up a tool, I consciously align my energy with the task at hand, realizing that the impact of my touch extends beyond the physical transformation. As practitioners of Reiki say, "Be present," but in my world of hair, it translates to "Be intentional."

This connection to energy is vital, for I am not merely crafting outer appearances; I am facilitating transformation from the inside out. With every snip, brush, hair wash or blow-dry, I allow my energy to flow. When that connection occurs, my tools become imbued with the shared energy of healing and beauty. This is the essence of the alchemy I practice, transforming hair into an embodiment of empowerment.

In closing this exploration of tools, I reflect on my journey as Kadybeauty and the unique relationship I forge with each instrument I use. They are not mere possessions; they are friends, teachers, and conduits of energy. Each moment spent with these tools taming hair into art, using brushes to apply color, or employing the warmth of a dryer to create a style becomes a sacred ritual infused with intention.

Just as in Reiki, where energy must be nurtured and respected, my tools thrive within a space filled with love and care. This commitment to my craft and my clients shapes not just the physical results of my work, but the emotional landscape of each appointment. By sharing my intimate relationship with these tools, I hope to deepen your understanding of the artistry behind hairdressing a dance of energy, connection, and beauty.

My tools are extensions of me, dancing harmoniously within the sacred space I have created. They tell the stories of the transformations I help facilitate, echoing the laughter, tears, and moments of growth that unfold within these walls. As I continue to master my craft, I remain committed to using these instruments not just to sculpt hair, but to nurture souls, creating a legacy of beauty and healing with every passerby through my doors.

Techniques and Styles

Kady stood in her salon, an alchemical space where creativity mingled seamlessly with healing energy. The scent of essential oils wafted through the air, mingling with the soft notes of Quran verses playing in the background, creating an ambiance ripe for transformation. Today, she was ready to share her journey through hair, highlighting the signature styles that had come to define her artistry and the techniques that brought them to life.

With each new day, Kady approached her craft like a painter with a fresh canvas. She often started by envisioning a style before even touching a strand of hair. Inspiration could strike from anywhere: the vibrancy of a street mural, the colors of an African sunset, or the intricate patterns found in nature. For Kady, every style had a story and emotion that she intended to evoke in the person sitting before her. Her first client of the day, Aisha, was a testament to that connection.

Aisha entered the salon with a look of uncertainty in her eyes. Her curls framed her face but seemed to lack direction and purpose. Kady immediately recognized the potential hidden within that naturally beautiful hair. "What do you feel when you look in the mirror?" she asked gently, drawing Aisha into the emotional currents that accompanied her appearance.

"I just feel... lost," Aisha confessed, her voice barely above a whisper. "I don't know what to do with my hair anymore."

This vulnerability tugged at Kady's heart. "Let's create a look that makes you feel strong and empowered. We can accentuate those wonderful curls and breathe new life into your hair," she replied, her tone filled with warmth. As they began, Kady's mind turned to the techniques she would employ, aiming to create a style that resonated with Aisha's inner strength.

Kady reached for her beloved curling wand, a tool that had turned many a mundane hairstyle into a masterpiece. She started by sectioning Aisha's hair into manageable parts. As she twirled each strand around the wand, Kady infused the movement with intention, reminding herself that energy and creativity flowed through her hands. Aisha watched in awe as her curls transformed from frizzy and chaotic to bouncy and defined.

"Wow, I didn't even know my hair could do this!" Aisha exclaimed, her smile broadening as each curl strutted into place. Kady couldn't help but share in her excitement the joy of seeing someone rediscover their beauty was unmatched.

Next came the finishing touches. Kady opted for a lightweight defining cream to enhance the curls while maintaining their integrity. "It's all about working with the natural texture," Kady explained, her fingers dancing through the newly crafted curls. With each manipulation of Aisha's hair, Kady invited her to visualize the strength of a lioness, a creature that embraced its wildness. By the time they were finished, Aisha no longer felt lost; she felt transformed.

The emotional journey intertwined with the physical process was what made Kady's work truly transformative. Each hairstyle told its own story, but they were all anchored in the core principle of connection. Kady considered how this approach aligned perfectly with her Reiki practice, reminding her that beauty was not merely an aesthetic but a holistic experience.

As she moved through the day, Kady reflected on her signature styles, each built upon a foundation of traditional techniques interwoven with contemporary flair. One of her favorite looks was the Braided Halo, a whimsical style that turned the mundane into something ethereal. The technique involved sectioning the hair, creating a fishtail braid that entwined elegantly around the crown, creating a halo effect that was as much about craftsmanship as it was about the energy Kady infused into it.

Kady recalled a time when Clara, a bride-to-be, sat nervously in her salon chair, unsure about how she wanted to present herself on her special day. With the weight of expectation hanging in the air, Kady envisioned the Braided Halo would accentuate Clara's features while embodying her dreams of a whimsical fairy-tale wedding.

"Let me show you something," Kady said, her voice laced with enthusiasm. She began sectioning Clara's hair while she shared anecdotes of how fairytales and timeless tales inspired her creations. Clara's smile deepened, her anxiety dissipating with the warmth of Kady's words.

As they moved through the styling process, the creation evolved beyond hair; it became a dialogue, a masterclass in trust and emotion. Kady gently wove the strands into place, her fingers firmly yet delicately tucking each braid into place. The warmth of her hands, combined with Clara's laughter and stories, created an essence of companionship that elevated the experience.

Kady designed the halo to hold light as if it possessed a magical aura, which is precisely what her clients radiated when Kady finished styling them. When Clara finally gazed into the mirror, the tears cascading down her cheeks were not merely reflections of surprise but joy and relief. "I've never felt so beautiful."

Kady knew that hairdressing wasn't just an art form it was a blend of love, stories, and connection. Each hairstyle was like an intricate piece of jewelry to be worn with pride.

Pushing the boundaries of her artistry, Kady also ventured into the world of color. It was not enough for her merely to cut and style; she craved to create dimension and intrigue. Using balayage techniques, Kady could paint strands of hair to catch the light, giving her clients a sun-kissed glow that was as radiant as their spirits.

One such client was Rina, a young woman on the cusp of significant life changes. As Rina sat in the chair, Kady sensed the weight of uncertainty in her heart. "I want a change, but I'm not sure how bold I can go," Rina admitted, her fingers nervously twisting a lock of her hair.

Kady took a moment to breathe deeply, centering her energy and harnessing the intuition she'd cultivated through her Reiki practice. "What if we add a touch of caramel to frame your face? The contrast will resemble warmth, reflecting your vibrant spirit." Rina's eyes widened, a hint of excitement igniting her features. Kady could feel the shift in energy, and with confidence, they began the transformation.

As Kady mixed the dye, she contemplated the alchemy of hair and healing. Color became a universal language, a way for her clients to express who they were and who they wanted to be. This gentle dance of color began painting a new era in Rina's life. With each stroke,

Kady shared her understanding of color theory, illustrating how different hues could reflect different emotions greater depth to an already vibrant personality.

When it came time to reveal the result, Kady instructed Rina to turn toward the mirror. Gasps echoed between them as Rina beheld her newfound self a radiant blend of sunlit caramel flickering against her natural chocolate locks. The transformation was not merely physical; it resonated deeply with Rina's spirit. "I've found my voice," Rina exclaimed, her eyes shining with renewed vigor, and Kady's heart swelled with joy.

Yet, amid these stories of triumph and beauty, Kady found herself faced with a challenge that would test and ultimately refine her skills. Enter Kendra, an ambitious entrepreneur who came to Kady with a vision one that seemed almost unattainable. Kendra desired to have her hair styled in a way that was both edgy and sophisticated, a reflection of her confident yet multifaceted character.

"This look needs to convey power," Kendra asserted from the moment she sat down. "Something modern, but still retains a kind of timeless grace."

Kady felt the weight of the request, recognizing both the beauty and complexity of what Kendra sought. This challenge became an opportunity for Kady to push her own boundaries. "I envision a high-contrast pixie cut," she suggested, her voice steady but infused with anticipation.

The decision, however, would not come without hurdles. As Kady began the transformation process, she worked meticulously with her scissors and clippers. The strands fell softly onto the salon floor like autumn leaves and the tangible manifestation of each cut marking a shift. Yet Kendra continued to feel uneasy, observing the radical change with skepticism that the outcome wouldn't live up to her vision.

Kady, ever attuned to the energies in the room, sensed the tension that began to creep in, threatening to hinder the creative flow. She paused, meeting Kendra's gaze in the mirror. "I know this might feel scary, but trust me this is a representation of your inner strength. Let's embrace the change together."

Reassured, Kendra took a deep breath, allowing Kady to continue. With every snip of hair, Kady infused her intent into the style: a promise of empowerment, a vow of authenticity. Kady played with the asymmetry of the cut, ensuring it was both daring and elegant, a visual representation of Kendra's spirit.

Finally, as she completed the look with bold highlights that danced around Kendra's face, Kady felt a deep sense of satisfaction in the outcome. She turned Kendra toward the mirror, and what was once uncertainty transformed into unabashed delight. The pixie cut framed Kendra's face with an audacious flair, and the gentle waves added an element of sophistication, striking the balance she longed for.

"I feel like a goddess!" Kendra beamed, her confidence emanating like a beacon around her. That moment became a shared victory, reinforcing Kady's belief in the powerful connection of hairdressing as a transformative art.

Through her signature style, Kady's journey served not only as a testament to her skills but as a profound reminder of the stories each client carried their narratives interwoven through every twist, color, and cut. In navigating these emotional landscapes, Kady realized that the art of hairdressing had become a beautiful dance between tradition and innovation, empowerment and trust.

As she reflected on her evolving practice, she discovered that pushing boundaries only deepened her appreciation for the roots of her craft. Each hairstyle remained grounded in respect for tradition, yet celebrated the individuality of each client. And as she closed the day, she felt invigorated, ready to welcome the next client into her sanctuary, into the sacred space where transformation occurred, one strand at a time.

The Connection with Clients

As I stand behind the salon chair, the familiar scent of shea butter and floral shampoo fills the air, enveloping me in a comforting embrace. It's in this serene space that I have the privilege of forging deep connections with my clients, transforming their hair and, often, their lives. Hairdressing is not just about the aesthetics of a cut or the perfection of a braid; it transcends technique. It is an art that thrives on relationship building, the intimate exchanges that occur when someone trusts you to not only style their hair but also to touch their very essence.

Every appointment tells a story, and I'd like to share a few that highlight the significance of these connections. One recurring figure in my life is Zara, a spirited young woman with curls that danced like wildflowers in the breeze. Zara first walked into my salon nearly three years ago, her expression revealing both excitement and trepidation. She was preparing for an important job interview, and the anxiety of the future clung to her like a wet cloak. As she seated herself in the chair, I could sense her nervous energy.

"Hello dear Queen, I'm Kady! What are you envisioning for your hair today?" I asked, smiling to ease her tension.

"I... I don't really know," she replied, her voice barely above a whisper. "I just want something that makes me feel confident."

I nodded, instantly aware that this appointment would entail more than just a transformation of her appearance. I offered her a warm, reassuring smile and began the process by engaging her in conversation, allowing her to unburden some of her worries about the interview.

As I brushed through her curls, I listened intently, asking questions about her aspirations, her interests, and the things that light her up. We talked about her love for painting and how she was seeking a job in graphic design. With each snip of the scissors, I sensed her confidence begin to blossom. I infused my work with intention, each cut a physical representation of the doubts she was shedding.

"Sometimes, we just need to let go of what weighs us down," I said softly, pausing to look into her eyes, which sparkled with hope.

In that moment, Zara's vulnerability shone through. Her worries about the interview, about being good enough, started to dissipate with each strand of hair that fell to the floor. By the end of our session, the revelation dawned on her that the power to stand out lay not in the perfection of her hair but in embracing her true self. As I styled the final touches, I saw her reflection in the mirror, a woman emerging with vibrant curls framed around her face, embodying newfound self-assurance.

"You look amazing! Are you ready to take on the world?" I asked, my heart swelling with pride.

"Thank you, Kady," she replied, her voice now strong and unwavering. "I feel like I can do anything!"

That was the beginning of a beautiful rapport. Zara visited me regularly, and with each appointment, our connection deepened. The salon transformed from a mere space for grooming into a sanctuary where she felt safe to share her dreams, fears, and milestones. I became her confidante, a trusted ally who could uplift her spirit simply by the act of trimming her curls or applying a fresh color.

One session stood out vividly in my memory Zara had recently been promoted at work after impressing her boss during the interview I had helped her prepare for. She walked in wearing a radiant smile that lit up the entire salon.

"I did it, Kady!" she exclaimed, her eyes glistening with excitement. "I got the job!"

Her enthusiasm was absolutely contagious. I could hardly contain my excitement as I spun her chair to face the mirror. "I always knew you had it in you!"

As I began to layer her hair, she kept talking, recounting her first week on the job, and the challenges she faced. "It's so much different than what I expected. Sometimes I feel like I don't belong there, like I'm not as skilled as my colleagues."

I paused momentarily, placing my scissors down. "Zara, remember where you started. You turned your uncertainties into strengths. Every hair you let fall today is testament to your growth."

With each layer I cut, I sensed the weight of her insecurities lifting. The transformation wasn't just physical; it was deeply emotional. By the end of our appointment, she looked radiant, her hair cascading beautifully down her shoulders, and her face aglow with confidence.

This cycle of connection grounded my work. Many clients entered the salon facing battles unseen, yet it was there that they found the courage to reveal their vulnerabilities. I would often reflect on how I became a vessel for their healing journeys, forging a safe harbor where trust floated freely.

One evening, after a long day of back-to-back appointments, a new client named Linda came in. Linda's eyes mirrored a profound weariness, framed by dark circles that tugged on my heart. As she settled into the chair, I felt compelled to dig deeper than the surface.

"Hello dear Queen! What brings you in today?" I asked gently.

"I'm getting married soon," she responded, her voice barely audible. "But I just lost my mom, so it's been tough to feel excited about anything."

A hush fell over the salon as I absorbed her words. This wasn't just a hair appointment; this was a moment of vulnerability steeped in grief and love. I shared my own story of loss, how it had shaped my understanding of beauty and the impermanence of life.

"Your mom will always be a part of you, and I believe she would be proud to see you embrace the joy of this occasion." I said, as I started to brush through her hair.

We worked together to create an updo that honored her mother's legacy while celebrating her love story. I adorned her hair with delicate white flowers, painstakingly weaving them throughout the hairstyle with love and intention. As we worked, I listened as she shared memories of her mother, each story adding layers of complexity to the rich tapestry of her life.

"What I've learned is that in celebrating love, we also celebrate the lives of those we hold dear," I remarked, emotional yet steadfast in my intention. "Let this be a joyful remembrance."

When Linda finally looked in the mirror, her face mirrored a fragile beauty, a mix of nostalgia and hope. "Thank you, Kady. I feel closer to her and to myself," she whispered, her voice breaking as tears welled in her eyes. She showed me her mother's photograph! I'm my mother's daughter with a smile.

In that moment, I realized the transformative power of connection within the salon. It was no longer merely about styling hair; it was about creating a space for emotional expression, where healing could transpire through shared experiences.

The stories don't end there; they continue to weave throughout the fabric of my salon. I recall an elderly client named Mabel who would come in weekly. Each appointment was filled with laughter and nostalgia, as Mabel regaled me with tales of her youth, including stories from her adventures in fashion. Together, we would explore daring hairstyles and colors that reflected her vibrant spirit.

One day, I suggested a bold plum hue. Mabel's eyes widened as she stammered, "At my age? But what will people think?"

"Let people think what they will," I encouraged, my heart racing with excitement. "This is about *you*! Let your hair be an expression of your vivacious spirit. You deserve to feel beautiful, no matter your age!"

With a tremor of excitement, she agreed, and as I dyed her hair, our conversation meandered through life's twists and turns. Mabel became a living testament to the idea that beauty is ageless. Her delight was infectious, and I would frequently see her out and about in the community with her new look, radiating confidence and joy.

Our appointments were filled with mutual respect and admiration, as we shared lessons of love, loss, and laughter. Mabel's transformation became another example of how our salon served as a conduit for healing and celebration. My connection with her also reminded me of the importance of honoring one's own self through the passing of time.

These stories reflect the essence of my work as both a hairdresser and a healer. Each client brings a unique energy, and it's within that energy exchange that the most profound transformations occur. The trust forged between us becomes a sacred bond, allowing us to peel back layers, revealing beauty hidden beneath the surface.

With each client that finds their way into my chair, I often remind myself of the importance of being present. It is easy to rush through appointments, focused on technique and speed; however, when I embrace the moment, every appointment becomes an opportunity for growth both for my clients and for myself.

There are times when I sense clients struggling, caught up in their battles. The connection we establish allows for healing energy to flow freely between us. I often invite clients to take a moment to breathe, to reconnect with themselves. The fundamental lesson I take away is that in transforming another's hair, I am equally transforming their spirit, a shared journey illuminating the truth in our vulnerability.

My own growth has mirrored that of my clients. Each story intertwines with my own, a vibrant tapestry of shared experiences that breathe life into the salon. I've learned to celebrate their victories, to grieve their losses, and to cherish the beautiful connection we've created. Wherever they are on their journey, I've become not just a hairdresser but also a trusted companion, committed to nurturing their transformation while flourishing with them.

Here's Clara's testimony

"I've been going to Kady for almost 10 years now, and I can confidently say that she changed not just my hair but my confidence, my self-expression, and my relationship with my identity.

When I first went to Kady, my hair was in shambles. I was a teenager who didn't know how to embrace my Black hair. I would straighten it wet or dry, bleach it with peroxide (terrible, I know), and had no idea how to care for it. At one point, due to my neglect, my hair became so matted that I spent days detangling it during my summer break. I legitimately hated my hair.

It was my mom who introduced me to Kady. At the time, my mom was getting box braids and twists, and suggested I give it a try. I was scared of change and hesitant about getting my hair done, but I agreed on one condition: I wanted color.

Little did I know, that one decision would be the first step toward learning to love my hair, growing my confidence, and discovering a whole new way to express myself.

Kady encouraged me to choose any color I wanted. We decided on burgundy hair with silver highlights, styled in box braids and they were beautiful. Everyone loved my hair, but more importantly, for the first time since I was a child, I loved my hair.

From there, we got bolder. After the burgundy and silver, we tried all-white hair. Over the years, we experimented with blue, purple, and rainbow highlights on top of the white. We went half-pink, half-blue. Then half-lilac and blue, all-blue, neon green faux locs, light blue, and now, I have half baby blue and half silver knot-less braids.

Kady's work truly speaks for itself. People are constantly drawn to my hair strangers stop me all the time to ask questions like, "How long did it take?" and "How often do you get it done?" But even more often, women tell me, "I could never pull that off."

They never mean it negatively. What they're really saying is they don't feel confident enough to express themselves that boldly.

It's always made me wonder when did we, as people, relinquish the freedom to express ourselves simply because we're concerned with what others might think?

Colored hair doesn't make someone less professional. Colored hair doesn't change someone's character. If someone is kind and friendly, having pink or blue hair doesn't change that. If someone is rude and mean, it's not because of the color in their hair.

We live in a world where trends are easy to follow and judgment is only a click away. In times like these, knowing who you are is so important.

For me, my identity is rooted in Christ. From that foundation, I have the freedom to express myself boldly and uniquely.

Thanks to Kady, I found the courage to embrace who I am today and the beauty that was always there.

- Clara Solomon"

As I reflect upon these experiences, I realize that my purpose transcends just hairdressing; I am a bridge connecting individual stories to a greater narrative of healing, self-expression, and love. Each haircut, style, or color has become an intimate expression not just of aesthetics, but of mutual understanding and compassion a symphony of shared journeys that resonates far beyond the confines of my salon.

The essence of my work lies within these moments, the alchemy of trust, growth, and resilience, where each hair appointment serves as a beautiful reminder that we are all inextricably connected, bound by the shared experiences that color our lives. It is this connection that defines my artistry, revealing the deeper layers of beauty that are more than skin deep. It beckons me to honor each individual journey while continuing to evolve my own, as I embrace my ever unfolding path as Kadybeauty the alchemist of hair and healing.

Reiki/ The Healing Touch

Understanding Reiki

Reiki, a practice that has fascinated and transformed countless lives, is rooted in the ancient traditions of Japan. Its name, derived from the Japanese words "rei," meaning universal, and "ki," meaning life energy, establishes the essence of this healing modality: a profound connection to the vital force that flows through each of us. From its origins with Mikao Usui in the early 20th century, Reiki has woven its way into the tapestry of modern healing practices, acting as a bridge between the physical and spiritual realms. As I began to explore the concept of Reiki, I found myself not only captivated by its potential for transformation but also confronted by my own doubts and challenges.

The journey into Reiki can oftentimes feel like stepping into a world where conventional beliefs about healing are challenged. For many practitioners and healers, the energy dynamics of Reiki can seem intangible; yet, as I delved deeper into the practice, I discovered that understanding these principles is key to harnessing their power effectively. At its core, Reiki embodies the idea that all living beings are interconnected through an invisible thread of energy that flows within and around us. This life energy is influenced by emotions, experiences, and the environment.

As I began to immerse myself in the principles of Reiki, I was introduced to its three primary tenets: acknowledgment of the life force energy, the notion of balance, and the practice of healing through guided intention. These concepts formed the foundation of my early learning. I began to conceptualize Reiki not as an abstract force, but as a tangible touchstone for promoting wellness both for myself and others.

It was during my first encounter with a seasoned Reiki master that I truly began to appreciate the intricacies of this practice. Entering her serene space, I was enveloped by a tranquil atmosphere enriched with gentle scents of essential oils and soft instrumental music in the background. My initial skepticism was palpable, evident in my furrowed brow and tense posture as I sat cross legged on a cushion, preparing for what I hoped would be a meaningful experience.

The Reiki master introduced the basic concepts with kindness and patience, emphasizing that everyone has the ability to channel healing energy if only we allow ourselves to tap into it. She shared with me the pivotal concept of energy flow, explaining how blockages can lead to physical and emotional distress. As she lightly placed her hands above my head, a rush of warmth enveloped me, like sunshine breaking through clouds after a storm. My skepticism began to melt away, replaced by an intriguing curiosity about this unseen force.

As I embarked on my path to becoming attuned to Reiki, I confronted personal struggles that mirrored the very challenges my clients would later reveal during our sessions. Self-doubt crept in like a stubborn shadow, and I often found myself questioning my ability to harness such a profound and invisible energy. Would I truly be able to channel this life force effectively? What if I made a mistake and my efforts caused harm instead of healing?

While I grappled with these insecurities, I also began to experience breakthroughs that would solidify my understanding of Reiki. During one particularly revelatory session, I worked with a client named Leila, a vibrant woman bursting with creative energy yet burdened with chronic anxiety. As I began the practice, I felt waves of energy surging through me, tinged with her apprehensions and fears. It was as though I became a vessel for her emotions. I guided my hands above her, following the flow of energy, and found that each slight adjustment elicited reactions in her body tremors, deep breaths, and at times, tears.

After that session, I realized that Reiki was as much about surrendering to the process as it was about active engagement. My initial hesitations faded, replaced by clarity and a sense of connection to not only my clients but also to a broader universal energy. In the days that followed, I continued refining my practice, implementing grounding techniques and visualization exercises that opened my heart to the flow of energy. I envisioned a warm light radiating from my palms, enveloping my clients and creating a cycle of healing where energy flows both ways.

Yet with every success came the ever-present challenge of skepticism surrounding Reiki, which can often be rooted in misconceptions that obscure its potential. I often encountered individuals who dismissed energy work as mere placebo or dismissed my abilities as mere theatrics. Some believed it to be a trend, a shortcut to healing that lacked scientific basis. I understood their perspectives; after all, we live in a world where furthering our understanding of the physical body predominates our notions of health and wellness. They preferred concrete, measurable solutions to their challenges relying on traditional medicine and therapy for answers.

In addressing this skepticism, I turned to my own journey of understanding. I realized that although Reiki may not fit neatly into conventional frameworks, its impact could undeniably be measured through the changes experienced by those who receive it. The soothing nature of a Reiki session often leads individuals to experience stress reduction, enhanced relaxation, and emotional release. As I shared anecdotes of clients who had embraced this practice, skeptics often leaned in, intrigued by the tangible outcomes rather than the principles underlying it.

One of my most profound experiences happened with a beloved friend named Amina, who had been grappling with a long-standing issue of self-acceptance. While talking to her one afternoon, I sensed a colossal barrier an energetic heaviness hovering above her heart. Amina had always been an unwavering support system for me, yet in that moment, I could see the internal struggle she faced, and it deeply affected my own heart. I suggested trying a Reiki session together, hoping to address the emotional distress manifesting in her body.

Initially hesitant, Amina acquiesced, and through our session, we discovered the layers of emotions routing her insecurities. As I worked through the energy blocks, Amina started to release what weighed her down. I witnessed her transformation in real-time. When she finally broke through her emotional barriers, the uplift in her spirit was palpable like a flower blooming after a harsh storm.

Through such experiences, I understood that skepticism often arises from a lack of awareness and exposure. In my perception, I sought not just to perform energy work but to cultivate understanding and acceptance of the benefits Reiki may bring. I would often describe to clients that Reiki is not a replacement for traditional medicine; rather, it can complement and enhance their healing journeys, guiding them to a balanced state of well being the very harmony for which we all strive.

As I deepened my understanding of Reiki, my perspective on energy itself transformed. I came to realize that energy is omnipresent a gentle continuum that fosters our shared existence. Just as we share a collective emotional experience in our interaction with others, we are all tuned into the same energy currents that flow through us. I began employing the practice of mindfulness, cultivating an awareness of my thoughts and feelings, recognizing how they influenced my energy and the energies of those around me.

Through my own trials and triumphs whether it was self-doubt, navigating societal skepticism, or facilitating healing in others I witnessed again and again the profound truth of Reiki: healing is an incredibly personal journey, and understanding its core principles offers an invitation to embrace not only its transformative potential but also the reshaping of our lives toward balance.

As I invite you to explore the principles of energy work, I hope you too will recognize its sacred beauty and embrace the foundational concepts that lie at its heart. Reiki teaches us that we have the power to channel this energy and become conduits of healing not only for ourselves but for those around us who seek solace and comfort. It reminds us that healing is rarely a solitary act; instead, it is a tapestry of connection and shared experience woven through every interaction filled with compassion and intention.

In summary, the essence of Reiki is a journey toward understanding an embrace of energy that flows through each of us, intertwined with the fabric of existence. Through my own experiences and reflections, I have come to see that the path to acceptance is layered with openness, compassion, and a willingness to explore the unseen. It is not merely the act of channeling energy, but the humble acknowledgment that we are part of a greater whole a collective tapestry of healing that nurtures both body and spirit. In shedding the misconceptions surrounding Reiki, we allow ourselves to embark on a journey toward deeper understanding, acceptance, and the abundant healing that awaits us.

Reiki in Practice

As Kady stood in her salon, she allowed herself a moment to simply breathe in the atmosphere she had worked so hard to cultivate. The gentle notes of calming Qur'an recitation floated through the air, mingling with the aromatic fragrances of essential oils and herbal infusions wafting from a diffuser in the corner. Soft lighting bathed the room in a warm glow, casting delicate shadows that danced with the flicker of candle flames strategically placed throughout the space. To her, this was more than just a salon; it was a sanctuary where beauty and healing converged, where transformations unfolded not just on the outside, but deep within the soul.

Kady understood that each client who sat in her chair was not just seeking a new hairstyle; they were also seeking a moment of connection, respite from their busy lives, and perhaps even a soothing balm for their emotional wounds. The integration of Reiki into her practice had opened new dimensions of healing, allowing Kady to work on the spirit as much as on the strands of hair that flowed between her fingers.

Her approach to hairdressing transformed into a multi-layered experience the day she first incorporated Reiki techniques into her routine. She began by inviting her clients to participate in a brief grounding exercise before starting any session. This involved having them sit comfortably, closing their eyes, and taking several deep breaths. Kady would ask them to visualize a calming color enveloping them, a simple yet profound practice that grounded both of them in the present moment. As she guided them through this visualization, she would gently place her hands on their shoulders, allowing her energy to meld with theirs.

"Feel the weight of your day melt away," she softly encouraged. "Allow yourself to be here, just as you are."

Over time, Kady developed a structured yet fluid framework for integrating Reiki into her work. Once her client felt settled, she could begin the physical transformation. Kady would typically start by assessing the client's hair, observing not only the texture and condition but also the energy they radiated. It was an intuitive process; she often sensed areas of tension in the client's energy field that aligned with knots in their hair.

During cutting, coloring, or styling, she would maintain a flow of energy through gentle hand placements on the client's head, neck, and shoulders. She had learned over the years that touch could be as much about intention as it was about technique. Through her hands, she would channel healing energy, infusing it into her strokes and movements. With every snip of her scissors or glide of her brush, Kady infused her work with intention, intending to weave healing into each strand of hair.

One day, Esther, a long-time client arrived at the salon looking visibly distressed. Kady's heart sank as she noticed the weight of the world on Esther's shoulders. A recent divorce had taken a toll on her spirit, and Kady sensed that this appointment was not just about hair; it was about mending broken pieces.

"Let's take a moment to pause and breathe," Kady suggested, guiding Esther into the grounding exercise. As they inhaled and exhaled together, Kady could feel the tension slowly dissipating from the air. By the time they transitioned into the haircut, she felt a palpable shift in Esther's energy, a lightness replacing the heaviness.

Kady began cutting Esther's hair, each snip releasing not just split ends but layers of emotional burden. She felt instinctively drawn to hold space for her, placing her hand gently on Esther's back as she snipped away. "You are shedding more than just hair today," Kady murmured, "You're releasing what no longer serves you."

The conversation turned deeper, flowing effortlessly between hairdressing and healing as Esther opened up about her fears and dreams. Kady maintained an open heart and a listening ear, embodying the principle of Reiki that emphasizes connection. In that moment, Kady understood that the healing process wasn't limited to energy; it was also about emotional release and support.

The longer Kady practiced integrating Reiki into her appointments, the more she became aware of her own growth as a practitioner. Early on, she often felt unsure and questioned whether she was truly capable of helping her clients on a spiritual level. However, through trials and heartfelt connections, she discovered that true healing came not just from mastery of techniques but from her willingness to be vulnerable and honest in her interactions.

Kady began to consciously evaluate the energy she brought into each appointment. She understood that to create a space of healing, she had to align her own energy first. This often involved her own rituals before a workday began; moments to meditate, set intentions, and visualize the energy she wanted to share with her clients. In those quiet moments with herself, Kady established a strong foundation for the energy she would later exchange.

An important aspect of the healing experience was the environment itself. She noted how colors, scents, and even the arrangement of the furniture influenced the energy in her salon. Each morning, Kady took care to clear the space with sage or sweetgrass, inviting only those energies that fostered healing and positivity. She connected deeply with her environment, ensuring that it reflected the nurturing essence she hoped to provide during each session.

Kady also learned to engage her clients in the healing process by teaching them simple Reiki techniques they could use at home. She would often introduce them to self-reiki practices, encouraging them to visualize healing light flowing into their lives. "You have the power to connect with this energy, whenever you need it," she would tell them, empowering them to take their healing into their own hands.

One of Kady's memorable clients, Mia, was a young artist battling anxiety that had begun to stifle her creativity. During her initial consultations, Mia shared her struggles openly, expressing how she felt paralyzed in her work and fearful of sharing her art. Kady not only styled Mia's hair beautifully but also provided her with a safe space to explore her feelings.

Throughout the appointment, Kady deliberately infused Reiki energy into Mia's experience. She imagined bright golden light pouring through her hands and into Mia, envisioning each strand of hair as a connection between their energies. At one point during the session, Kady encouraged Mia to reflect on her dreams and the barriers that stifled her. "What if you allowed that light to shine through your work?" Kady asked, gently lifting Mia's chin to meet her gaze in the mirror.

To Kady's delight, she began seeing a transformative sparkle in Mia's eyes. The emotional release and energy exchange between them transformed the atmosphere, clearing the stagnation that had been inhibiting Mia's creativity.

By the time Mia's hair was styled into a chic bob, the heaviness that once draped over her shoulders had lifted. Upon catching a glimpse of her reflection, Mia gasped. "I feel…free!" she exclaimed, her voice quivering with excitement.

Kady smiled, her heart swelling with joy as she realized that their exchange had borne fruit. It was at that moment that Kady understood the dual nature of transformation within her practice; she was not just changing hair; she was connecting, inspiring, and healing.

As Kady continued weaving Reiki into her hairdressing, she often found comfort in the simple yet profound alignment of intention. Before every appointment, she would silently invite guidance and clarity, asking for the right words to connect with her clients deeply. Those moments of intention setting became as essential to her practice as her choice of scissors or shampoo.

With each client, she gathered lessons that could only be learned through the intimacy of shared experiences. From high-energy discussions to serene moments of silence, Kady recognized the beauty in duality the meeting of hairstyling and healing, interaction and introspection, vulnerability and strength.

As her reputation grew, so did her clientele. The energy exchange became richer as more clients reported feelings of lightness, clarity, and emotional release after appointments. Kady began documenting these shifts, collecting stories that revealed the deeper essence of her work. She started to recognize patterns in her clients' transformations, amplifying her understanding of the healing process. Each session was not just an appointment; it became a sacred ritual that deepened the connection between healer and client.

In Kady's journey of 'Reiki in Practice', her growth as a practitioner became a tapestry of compassion intertwined with skill. The clients who sat in her chair became partners in healing rather than mere recipients of beauty services.

Through each cut, color, and style, Kady knew she was shaping not just hair but also the narratives of the women and men who walked through her doors. She embraced her role not simply as a hairdresser but as a conduit for transformation and healing.

As the sun dipped below the horizon one evening after a fulfilling day, Kady took a moment to reflect on her journey. She realized that the purpose of her work integrating Reiki into hairdressing was about fostering love, support, and connection. It was about honoring the stories, struggles, and sacrifices of everyone who entered her space. Kady envisioned a vibrant future where her salon would continue to be a haven for those seeking not just beauty, but also healing.

With every appointment, Kady reaffirmed her commitment to her craft and clients, proud of the alchemy she had cultivated. "This is my calling," she whispered to herself. "A beautiful intertwining of hair and healing, art and energy." In that moment, surrounded by the soft embrace of her sanctuary, Kady felt inspired to continue her journey as both a hairdresser and a healer, bringing forth beauty that nourished the soul.

Energy Exchange

The salon buzzes with energy, a vibrant atmosphere filled with laughter, the gentle rustle of hair being styled, and the soft melodies of calming music that creates an inviting sanctuary for both clients and myself. In this sacred space, I understand that the act of hairdressing transcends mere aesthetics; it becomes an essential ritual of connection, of transformation. Each appointment is an opportunity to engage in an energy exchange, where the flow of healing energy between myself and my clients fosters mutual growth and renewal.

As I prepare for my day, I take a moment to center myself, to align my energy with the purpose of my work. I light a candle, infuse the room with the scent of essential oils, and take a few deep breaths to ground myself in the present. I remind myself that every thought, every intention, and every touch carries an energetic imprint that can influence the experience we are about to share. The ancient wisdom of Reiki teaches that energy flows where intention goes, and I am committed to harnessing that energy to create a healing environment for everyone who steps into my salon.

One of the most profound examples of energy exchange occurred with a client named Nina. When she first arrived at my salon, Nina was a young woman struggling with a deep sense of insecurity. Her once vibrant spirit was dulled by constant self-doubt, and she often kept her long, unruly hair tied back in a tight, unremarkable bun. As we exchanged pleasantries and she settled into the salon chair, I could feel the weight of her energy, heavy with unresolved pain and a yearning for change.

"Tell me about your hair," I asked, opening the door to a conversation that I hoped would reveal the layers of her story.

Nina hesitated, glancing at her reflection in the mirror. "I've never really liked it. It feels like it has a mind of its own. I just want it to look nice," she admitted, her voice barely above a whisper. With those words, I recognized the beginning of a journey not just to a new hairstyle, but to a renewed sense of self.

As I washed her hair, I took extra care to massage her scalp, allowing the warm water and nourishing shampoo to wash away not only the dirt and grime but the energy that had been stifling her spirit. As tension began to dissipate, I felt the shift in the energy between us a gentle tug, an opening, a moment where the air felt charged with possibility.

"Do you have any ideas for what you'd like to do?" I inquired, hoping to ignite a spark of inspiration within her.

"I've always admired curly hairstyles," she replied, her eyes lighting up for the briefest moment. "But I don't think I could ever pull them off."

The energetic exchange began to reveal itself. As we discussed different curly styles, I felt warmth radiating from her, and I could sense that beneath her hesitations lay a burgeoning desire to express her true self. "Each curl can be a symbol of your uniqueness," I shared, drawing parallels between the freedom of style and the freedom of spirit. "It's about embracing who you are, in all your beautiful complexity."

With each snip of the scissors and twist of her hair, I infused my intention into the process, visualizing growth and healing intertwining with each layer I cut away. In that moment, I felt the deep connection between us the subtle interplay of energies where my intention met her readiness to change. She spoke freely now, expressing her hopes and fears, her laughter filling the room as we grew more comfortable with one another.

By the time I finished her transformation, Nina looked in the mirror, her breath catching in her throat. The curls danced around her face, framing her features in a way that spoke of freedom and confidence. The energy shifted dramatically, her earlier heaviness replaced with a buoyancy that radiated outwards. In that instant, the energy exchange became clear: I had channeled my own healing energy into her transformation, while in return, she gifted me her vulnerability and trust.

"I feel... incredible," she whispered, tears glistening in her eyes. "I didn't know I could look like this."

That exchange of energy, her joy mingling with my intention was a profound reminder of the power of mutual healing. It dawned on me that through the simple act of hairdressing, we not only transformed hair but discovered the beauty of healing connections. Each client coming into my space wasn't just seeking a new hairstyle; they were seeking validation and empowerment.

As Nina left the salon, her strides were lighter, her head held high, and I felt a renewed sense of purpose. But it's not always as straightforward. The energy exchanges are complex and not every client walks out transformed in the same way. There are days when I encounter clients who carry the weight of their battles more heavily than others.

Another client, Marissa, came to me one overcast afternoon. She was a woman in her late forties, her hair marked by years of struggle and stress that were etched into her very being. As she settled into the chair, her energy felt closed off, defensive a protective layer that had been thickened by years of disappointment.

"I've just been through a really rough time," she shared, her voice trembling slightly. "I lost my job, and I don't know how I'm going to pay my bills. I don't really feel like myself anymore."

I nodded, recognizing her pain and the heaviness that radiated from her. As I began to wash her hair, I made it intentional to connect with her energy, silently sending out waves of compassion and understanding. "Let's take a moment to breathe together," I suggested, encouraging her to close her eyes. "Inhale deeply, and as you exhale, imagine releasing the weight you're carrying."

As her breaths grew deeper, I felt layers of tension begin to peel away, and I was reminded of the profound impact that simply being present can have. In that space, I became the vessel for her to release her burdens, even if only momentarily. With each wash, I invited healing energy to flow between us, again being mindful of my intention. I wanted her to move beyond the external beauty we were creating to touch places deeper within her.

"What about a fresh start?" I asked as I styled her hair, suggesting a bold color change alongside a trendy cut that symbolized renewal. "Sometimes, the outside transformation can mirror what's happening within."

As Marissa looked at herself in the mirror with disbelief, a flicker of hope ignited in her eyes. "I didn't think this was possible," she whispered, a smile breaking through her tears.

"I did," I responded, feeling the energetic shift between us; the walls she had built around her soul were beginning to soften. By honoring her journey and supporting her through a pivotal moment, we both experienced a profound exchange the healing was reciprocal, with both of us involved in an intricate dance of energy.

In those moments, I often find myself reflecting on the emotional energy I carry and project. There are days when my own energy is low, vulnerable to the burdens I face in my life. It is crucial for me to engage in self-care practices, meditation, reiki training, and personal rituals to ensure that I channel only the best energy to my clients. Each appointment requires me to fully immerse myself, but it also demands self-awareness, as I cannot serve effectively if I do not honor my own needs.

The vast array of emotions I encounter in the salon joy, sorrow, anxiety, excitement are constantly intermingling. It's my responsibility to remain present and grounded, to let the negative energy slide away while embracing the positive. I remember a particular day when I had experienced a personal disappointment outside of the salon. I arrived feeling fragile, unsure of my energy reserves, when a longstanding client named Maria walked in.

Maria had been journeying through her own challenges, and our appointments often felt like shared healing sessions. "Kady," she sighed, sinking into the chair. "I can feel something's off with you. What's happening?"

I hesitated, wondering if I should share my troubles, but in her light hearted way, she encouraged me to speak freely. Standing together at that crossroad of vulnerability and support allowed us both to tap into a profound exchange. As I shared my feelings, Maria listened with an open heart, reflecting back the importance of resilience. By engaging in honest and authentic conversation, we both transformed the energy in the room.

As I styled her hair, Maria reciprocated with her own energy, uplifting me with her warmth and resilience. "Remember, Kady, we're a community here. You've been a light for me during my struggles, and I want to be a light for you too," she said. "Let's honor our journeys together."

In that moment, I understood the essence of energy exchange: it was a mutual collaboration, a dance of give and take, where the healing was not one sided but a beautiful, resonant circle. By allowing ourselves to be vulnerable and genuine, we open the door for reciprocal growth and healing.

The testimonials from my clients serve as illuminating markers of the energetic exchanges we create. After a transformative appointment, I often receive heartfelt notes and messages that recount their experiences. One particular message from Sofia stands out: "Kady, I walked into your salon feeling invisible. When I looked in the mirror after our time together, I saw a woman reborn. You didn't just style my hair; you breathed life into my spirit. Thank you for your healing touch."

Those words resonate within me, affirming the power of connection. They remind me that the energy I channel transcends the hair itself; it is about engaging in a sacred ritual of transformation, acceptance, and love. I cherish these testimonials, as they are reminders of the mutual energy exchange my gift to them and their gift back to me, intertwining our paths in this journey of healing.

Sometimes, there are clients who arrive feeling uncertain, reluctant to let down their barriers, and it's easy to sense their hesitance. One of them was Lia, who walked in wearing a mask of fear. "Can you promise me that this won't be another disappointment?" she asked, her skepticism palpable. It tugged at my heartstrings.

"No promises, but I can promise to pour my heart into this process," I replied, allowing authenticity to guide my words. "I want you to feel empowered, not just in how your hair looks, but how you feel inside. This is about more than just transformation; it's about awakening your innate beauty."

As I gently cradled her hair, I took the opportunity to connect her energy with mine. I reminded myself that sometimes, the best healing begins with patience. We spent the appointment exploring the depths of her story the dreams she had sidelined, the barriers she had placed, and the light she wished to reclaim.

By respecting the energy dynamics at play, we gradually moved past the initial hesitance, venturing into a realm of openness. When Lia finally looked in the mirror at her new look vibrant and rich with color she gasped. "Oh wow," she said, tears welling in her eyes. "I didn't think I could look like this."

As the tears spilled over, I embraced her in a moment of shared understanding. "You look beautiful because you allowed yourself to be seen," I whispered, feeling my own heart swell with emotion. In the next few minutes, we shared laughter, tears, and reflections, fully present in that sacred space, creating a profound synergy between us, one woven from trust and vulnerability.

In my practice, I strive to recognize the uniqueness of each client's journey and to honor that journey with intention and reverence. Each exchange transforms me, deepening my understanding of my own energy and illuminating the interconnectedness of our human experiences. I am continuously learning to navigate the ebb and flow of energies that crisscross within my salon.

As I reflect on these experiences, I feel a deep gratitude for the energy exchanges that unfold in this space of healing. Hairdressing, combined with the principles of Reiki, has gifted me so much more than just my craft; it has opened the door to a community of healing, where each appointment is an invitation to dive into shared stories a chance to explore the beautiful, dynamic interplay of energy that connects us all.

As I work with my clients, I am reminded that I am both a healer and a vessel of transformation. My hands are the conduits of energy that flow from my intention to their hair, manifesting a tapestry of healing for us to share. Together, we embrace the alchemy of hair and healing, forging connections that extend beyond the tools of my trade, transcending the physical realm and tapping into the deep, soulful essence of what it means to be alive, to be seen, and to be transformed.

The Sacred Ritual

Creating the Sacred Space

Kady stood at the threshold of her salon, taking a moment to breathe in the energy around her. The air hummed with potential, and she could feel the warm embrace of the sunlight filtering through the frosted glass windows. This was her sanctuary, where hair and healing intertwined seamlessly, where each appointment became a sacred ritual imbued with intention and love. Over the years, Kady had learned that the environment she created was as vital as the services she provided; it was essential for her clients to feel safe and celebrate the moment they walked through the door.

With each morning's first light, Kady followed a cherished routine that prepared her space for the transformative work ahead. There was an artistry to it, akin to a painter selecting hues for a masterpiece. She began by lighting her favorite incense, a blend of lavender and sage that filled the air with a calming, earthy aroma. The smoke curled gently toward the ceiling, carrying with it Kady's whispered prayers and intentions. "May this space be a haven of healing," she murmured, allowing her intentions to intermingle with the fragrant tendrils, hoping they would settle deep into the foundations of her salon.

The soothing scent wafted through the room, beckoning her to surrender to the tranquil atmosphere she was crafting. Kady understood the power of scent; it had the capacity to evoke memories and emotions, to ground her clients in the present moment. She remembered her grandmother dancing through their home while preparing her hair, the scent of shea butter and coconut oil mixing with laughter, warmth, and love. Kady wanted her clients to feel that same cherished connection to their own beauty, and scent was her starting point.

Next, she turned her attention to lighting. Kady preferred a combination of soft overhead fixtures complemented by flickering candles, which cast a gentle glow that wrapped around the room like a warm blanket. The transition from the harshness of fluorescent bulbs to the inviting warmth of her carefully curated lighting made all the difference. The salon's ambience soon morphed into something sacred. It became an oasis designed to soothe even the most frayed nerves. She adjusted the dimmers until the light felt just right bright enough to work, yet soft enough to promote relaxation and ease.

"Lighting is key," Kady often reminded her apprentice, who joined her in the salon on busy weekends. "It can transform a place from ordinary to extraordinary. Set the scene for healing, and the energy will flow."

As she arranged her styling station, Kady chose each tool with intention. Her scissors, brushes, and combs were arranged meticulously, a collection that represented years of learning, mastery, and deep personal connection. Each tool had its own story, a history woven into the fibers of their existence. The scissors belonged to an influential mentor, the brushes gifted by clients who admired her talent. They were infused with energy, carrying the whispers of those who had passed through her salon chair. Every decision she made in curating her space connected the past to the present, allowing those who entered to feel the weight of history and the promise of new beginnings.

The music started softly, a blend of calming piano melodies and gentle chimes designed to enhance the healing atmosphere. Kady carefully curated playlists that resonated with her own energy, creating a sonic landscape that supported deep relaxation. She favored artists whose compositions embraced the essence of tranquility, where each note felt like a caress. The music set a rhythm, drawing clients into an experience that transcended mere hairdressing. Here, they would embark on a journey of self-discovery and healing, with Kady as their guide.

In the background, the dim glow of fairy lights strung with care twinkled like stars overhead, while handmade decorations adorned the walls. Photographs of clients from previous transformations adorned one section, reminders of the joy and empowerment that arose from her artistic touch. Kady smiled at the faces immortalized in time, each one a story, a journey shared in sacred space. The salon walls acted as witnesses to countless tissue laden moments, from radiant laughter to tears of release.

To her, each object within the salon symbolized the power of creation and community. Plants adorned every corner, their deep green leaves adding a vibrancy that felt alive. Kady believed that nature offered a form of healing in its own right; she wanted a space where the clients felt grounded and connected to the earth. She had spent hours researching and selecting the right plants for her sanctuary, knowing that each brought its own energy, air purification, and vibrancy.

As she watered the peace lily, she recalled the conversations she had shared with clients beneath its lush leaves. It had become a site of sustenance and support, a living representation of growth. Nurturing the plants mirrored Kady's own commitment to nurturing her clients. "May we both continue to thrive," she whispered to the plant as she carefully poured water, each droplet a promise to honor the life within it.

Kady stepped back to admire her handiwork, her heart swelling with gratitude. Every detail felt intentional, woven together in service of something larger than herself. This wasn't just a salon; it was a dynamic healing space where conversations flowed freely, and connections were forged. Kady often reflected on how her clients came to her seeking more than just a new hairstyle; they arrived with hopes, dreams, and burdens. She carried the weight of their stories, understanding her role as both caretaker and artist; it was a delicate balance, one built on trust and authenticity.

Ultimately, it was the intention behind each gesture that transformed ordinary hairdressing into a sacred experience. Kady had learned through her Reiki training that energy was palpable, flowing through her hands, and she leaned into that knowledge each day. Every snip of the scissors or stroke of the brush was imbued with her focused intent; she viewed each appointment as a chance to share the healing energy she had cultivated both in the salon and herself.

Before the first client of the day arrived, Kady took a moment to center herself, inhaling deeply as she visualized the energy in the space aligning with her purpose. "May my hands be guided by love, and may my heart connect deeply with those who enter," she whispered quietly. The practice of breath was ingrained in her, allowing her to set the tone for the appointments that lay ahead.

It was in those soft moments that Kady felt most connected to the profound wisdom of her practice. "Each appointment is a collaboration," she often expressed. "We both come to the table clients seeking beauty, and I offer them a vessel to uncover it." With every breath, she welcomed the energy of possibility that hovered in the air, ready to mingle with the essence of her clients.

As the first sound of the doorbell rang, Kady turned her attention fully to the incoming energy. She welcomed each client with warmth and authenticity, remembering the importance of making them feel seen and heard. "Welcome," she said, her smile genuine as she motioned for them to step further inside. "You're home."

Transitioning into the realm of hair and healing was a dance of intent. Kady operated from the understanding that as she worked, the environment they shared was charged with transformative potential. In moments when she brushed hair and tucked loose strands behind ears, she recognized the nuances of touch and how deeply it resonated.

During hair appointments, she listened intently, not only to their words but also to the unspoken stories that often floated between them. The sacred space she created allowed clients to feel comfortable sharing their struggles, dreams, and vulnerabilities. She offered them space to express themselves freely, knowing that the act of sharing was itself a form of healing.

Under the soft glow of her carefully curated lighting, Kady encouraged conversations that might not occur in other settings conversations about self-love, acceptance, and transformation. "Our hair is a reflection of our identity," she often mused. "In changing our hairstyle, we can often change our perspective."

The sacredness of her salon resonated as a place of connection, healing, and artistry. It was where clients learned to embrace both their outer beauty and inner strength. They felt invited into a sacred ritual, one that transcended the physical transformation of their hair and led to the rejuvenation of their spirits.

As she worked, Kady's heart swelled knowing that cultivating airy tranquility and nurturing beauty would not only enhance individual experiences but ripple out into the wider community. Her salon became a nexus of healing an alchemical space where hairdressing transformed into an act of self-love, where laughter intertwined with prayer and intention.

With each appointment, Kady invited her clients to experience not just a change in hair but a profound shift in life. This embodied connection wasn't just for the moment spent in the chair; it became a foundation of trust as they left the sanctuary, empowered to take on the world.

The space they shared felt sacred, a temple where the mundane transformed into something extraordinary. She had created more than just a salon; she had established a community, a healing hub that echoed with stories, aspirations, and a promise of transformation. Each person who stepped into her sanctuary left with more than a new hairstyle; they carried with them a renewed sense of self.

Kady continued to nurture that sanctuary every day, remembering that it was not only the materials, tools, or atmosphere that made the salon special but the genuine connection she fostered with her clients.

As she tidied her tools and prepared for another day, Kady found herself deep in gratitude, realizing that in sharing her energy and creating a sacred space, she had tapped into something greater than herself. Her salon was alive with possibility, a living embodiment of the alchemy of hair and healing.

Rituals Before Appointments

Kady stood in her salon, the golden morning light filtering through the window, casting gentle rays across her workspace. The air was infused with the faint scent of essential oils, mingling with the nostalgic aroma of shea butter and coconut oil. To anyone else, this might seem like just another day in her bustling salon, but for Kady, it was a sacred beginning a prelude to the transformative experiences she would soon share with her clients.

As she began her day's preparations, she engaged in a series of personal rituals designed to ground her spirit and align her intentions. These acts were more than mere routines; they were an integral part of her practice that enriched the energy she brought into her salon. Kady understood that to facilitate healing and beauty for others, she first had to tend to her own emotional and spiritual well being.

Her first ritual began with a moment of silence. Kady settled into a comfortable seat, closed her eyes, and took a deep, cleansing breath. Inhale... and hold... The air filled her lungs with warmth, and the gentle rise and fall of her chest reminded her of life's rhythm. Exhaling slowly, she released the stresses of the world outside, freeing herself from the mental clutter that could disrupt the flow of energy during her appointments.

"Today, I invite positive energy," she whispered to herself, adding clarity to her intention. This simple affirmation served as a reminder to welcome each client with an open heart, ready to engage in a healing exchange. Breathing deeply, Kady envisioned her energy field expanding, creating a protective bubble around her, shielding her from any negativity as well as aligning her with the high frequency she wished to cultivate.

As a Reiki practitioner, Kady was no stranger to the power of intention and visualization. Each day before she began her work, she made a conscious effort to connect with her spirit guides and the energy of the universe. For her, it was crucial to tap into a higher frequency that resonated with her healing capabilities and the transformative journeys of her clients, who each carried unique energies waiting to be harmonized.

Sitting cross-legged on a soft mat in the corner of her salon, Kady picked up a handful of crystals from her collection that adorned a small wooden shelf nearby. Each stone held distinct properties, contributing to her energy work in unique ways. Today, she chose a rose quartz for love and compassion, amethyst for spiritual growth, and citrine for abundance and positivity. As she held them in her palms, she closed her eyes once more, mentally inviting their energies into her own.

She imagined the rose quartz radiating warmth, enveloping her in profound love and kindness, essential to her healing practice. The amethyst shimmered with spiritual insight, sharpening her intuition and decision-making abilities. Meanwhile, the citrine infused her with clarity and optimism, prompting her to share these qualities with each person that would step into her sanctuary.

Kady began to set her intentions for the day aloud as she held one crystal after another. "May I attract clients who are ready to embrace change," she declared, letting the vibrations of her voice intertwine with the energies of the stones. "May I guide them towards self-love and acceptance." Each affirmation became a prayer, enriched by her deep seated commitment to the art of hairdressing and healing.

Following her crystal meditation, Kady moved onto her next ritual: journal writing. Sitting at a small wooden desk adorned with colorful pens, she opened her notebook to a fresh page, preparing to pour her thoughts onto the paper. This practice served as a vehicle for clarity, allowing her to process emotions and solidify her intentions.

"Today, I welcome transformation," she wrote in bold strokes, followed by a list of actions she could take to connect with her clients during their appointments simple reminders to listen deeply, hold space, or offer healing touch. The rhythmic motion of her pen grounded her, serving as an anchor to the emotional currents that often surged within her as she prepared her salon for her clients.

Kady's mentor, a wise woman named Mama Juma, had taught her the significance of journaling as a part of her ritual. Mama Juma had been an integral presence in Kady's journey towards merging her hairdressing and Reiki practices. With a deep understanding of energy work and the traditions of their ancestors, she often emphasized the importance of reflection and intention-setting in cultivating one's practice.

"Meditation and journaling are essential," Mama Juma had advised her during one of their sacred conversations, the moonlight casting soft shadows around them as they shared stories of healing.

71

"When you write, dear Kady, you solidify your intentions and allow yourself to explore the depths of your soul. What emerges on the page must be honored and reflected in your work."

With her mentor's wisdom echoing in her mind, Kady closed her journal, feeling a sense of readiness coursing through her. She gathered the crystals, placing them back on the shelf as a gesture of appreciation for their contribution to her morning rituals. Each piece of this ritual had fortified her energy, elevating her presence and aligning her spirit for what lay ahead.

The final element of her pre-appointment ritual involved the carefully curated atmosphere of her salon. Kady understood that energy can be felt as much as it can be seen, and the environment she created played a crucial role in establishing a space conducive to healing. She moved gracefully through her salon, adjusting the lighting and placing fresh flowers on the countertops, their vibrant colors inviting positivity into the space.

With each smile and touch, Kady arranged the space to evoke harmony and comfort. She played soft ambient music a blend of gentle flutes and soothing rain sounds that filled the air without overwhelming the senses. The melodies wrapped around her, inviting a transformative energy that further relaxed her spirit.

"May this space be sacred," Kady whispered, her heart full of reverence as she lit a calming lavender incense stick, watching the smoke curl upward. "May everyone who enters feel at peace."

As she moved about the salon, Kady could almost sense the energy settling, enveloping the area in a tranquil embrace. With each ritual that coursed through her, she became increasingly aware of the importance of being present not just as a hairdresser but as a healer and an energy worker. It had become a natural part of her flow, where each client's journey connected with hers in ways that transcended mere hairdressing.

In the moments before her first appointment of the day, the salon filled gradually with clients seeking Kady's touch, each person stepping into her sacred space, brimming with their own energies and stories. She felt an overwhelming sense of gratitude for the trust they bestowed upon her.

It was a ritual within a ritual, this energetic dance between them. Kady found herself smiling, filled with anticipation as the bell above the door jingled, welcoming a bright-eyed woman named Sarah.

"Good morning, Sarah!" Kady greeted, her warmth radiating like the sun. The two embraced, a pause that connected their spirits. Kady took a moment to assess Sarah's energy, sensing an air of vulnerability mingled with eagerness a reflection she recognized in many clients.

"Are you ready for your transformation today?" she asked, her voice soft yet firm, inviting Sarah to share her feelings. The two settled into conversation, creating a safe space for vulnerability within Kady's sanctuary.

As Sarah spoke, Kady listened deeply, her heart and mind aligned with the intentions she had crafted earlier. She recounted her own struggles with self-acceptance and resonated with Sarah's experience, reflecting on their shared stories while remembering the power of connection. This moment not only enriched her understanding of Sarah but solidified the bond that Kady wanted to cultivate one where the energy exchanged became a healing experience for them both.

Taking a moment, Kady closed her eyes briefly as she began her process, binding her rituals together with a few affirmations as she spoke quietly. "We are safe. We are loved. We are transforming," she said, resonating with her earlier intentions and the vibrational essence of their connection.

The room felt softer as Kady prepared to work. She positioned her tools, mindful of their readiness and the energy inherent within them. She could feel the shifts taking place in the atmosphere, a palpable essence that ignited her spirit and charged the air with possibilities. With each brush of her fingers through Sarah's hair, she became increasingly aware of the vibrations—an exquisite balance of chemistry between their energies.

As her hands moved skillfully, Kady remained cognizant of the realm they had entered together: a sacred space woven with threads of beauty, vulnerability, and trust. The air vibrated subtly between them, a united force that instigated healing through layers of emotional expression, weaving a tapestry of transformation.

This is the essence of Kady's practice where rituals of self-care flowed seamlessly into the service she provided. Each entrusting soul who entered her salon became part of a greater narrative, one that resonated with authenticity and healing touch.

Later that evening, as Kady reflected on her day filled with energy exchanges and transformations, she once again found solace in her rituals. In this moment, she felt gratitude for Mama Juma's guidance, for the crystals that offered support, and for the wisdom of intention that infused every appointment with vibrancy and authenticity. The love and energy shared could ripple outward, creating waves of healing beyond her salon's walls, ushering kindness and self-empowerment into the broader community.

With a heart full of love and energy nourished by her rituals, Kady embraced the journey of being both a hairdresser and a healing spirit, forever grateful for the sacred connections forged through the simple yet profound act of caring for one another. The world outside was a cacophony of chaos, but inside her sanctuary, nestled in the essence of healing, Kady knew peace reigned.

The Healing Process

The atmosphere in my salon is intentionally curated, a delicate balance of tranquil sounds and subtle scents that create an oasis for my clients. Each appointment begins with a moment of silence, a shared breath where I invite my clients to settle into the space mentally and emotionally. As they take a seat in my chair, I observe the subtle nuances the way their shoulders may carry tension, the flicker of anxiety in their eyes, or the deep exhale that hints at the weight of their day. It is in these moments that I find the first signs of the healing journey, grounded in my role as both hairdresser and healer.

I begin by gently combing through their hair with my fingers, a ritual that serves as an anchor for both of us. The act of touch is sacred; it speaks a language beyond words. As I glide my fingers through their hair, I focus on finding the knots, both physical and emotional. Sometimes, a client's hair tells the story of their life broken ends reflecting broken dreams, tangled strands indicating accumulated stress. I approach each client's hair almost as a canvas, embedding my intention with each stroke while also being hyper-aware of the energy pulsing between us.

A client I recall vividly is Maya. She walked into my salon one rainy afternoon, her demeanor is heavy, radiating exhaustion. After we exchanged pleasantries, I invited her to close her eyes and take a few deep breaths. As my hands began to sift through her hair, I could feel the weight of her worries reverberating through her scalp. I asked her if she wanted to share what was on her mind, but I sensed her hesitation.

"Sometimes it's easier for me to talk about it while you work," she said, her voice barely above a whisper.

A smile crept across my face as I encouraged her to speak. I have always found that sharing this space the salon chair becomes a cocoon for release and rejuvenation. As I layered her hair, I felt her tension slowly dissipate like the mist that gathers after rain. With each pass of my scissors, I visualized us cutting away not only the dead ends of her hair but also the emotional burdens she carried. It was a practice of intention, where healing flowed seamlessly through touch and conversation.

Maya spoke of her recent breakup, the loneliness that clung to her like a dark cloud. All the while, I listened not just to her words but to the energy that shifted in the air. I sensed the raw vulnerability that accompanied her pain, feeling a pulse of sympathetic energy resonating within me. I softly encouraged her, weaving affirmations into our dialogue: "You're worthy of love. You are enough. This is just a chapter, not your whole story."

As I styled her hair into soft, gentle waves, I visualized love flowing toward her, gentle and affirming. I could see her visibly relax, her body unclenching as she shared memories of laughter and hope that still flickered brightly within her heart. We moved through shades of light and dark, as I guided her with love and intention. By the end. I stood back to reveal the final look, and her eyes sparkled with unexpected delight. It was as if our shared energy had breathed life back into her.

"Thank you, Kady," she said, a renewed brightness in her voice. "I came in feeling broken, and I left feeling whole."

This is the essence of the healing process that unfolds in my salon not merely the artistry of hairdressing but the alchemy of connection, where we both emerge transformed. Each client journey is uniquely woven, marked by the threads of personal transformation that intertwine their narratives with mine. This exchange goes beyond aesthetics; it is a journey of finding oneself amid the strands.

Another poignant experience occurred with a client named Jamal, who had been grappling with self-acceptance. A hairstylist himself, he was deeply familiar with the industry's pressures, often feeling he needed to fit into a mold that didn't honor who he truly was. While working on his hair a series of bold curls that framed his face he opened up about his struggles with identity.

"Sometimes I hate looking in the mirror," he remarked, his brow furrowed. "I see someone I'm not proud of."

Those words struck a chord within me. I paused, letting silence anchor us before I asked, "What would it look like if you embraced yourself fully?"

As I began to trim and shape his curls, I infused the process with deliberate intention, holding a vision of him confidently embracing his identity. I used each snip as a way to affirm his worth. "You are vibrant. You are unique. The world needs your light," became a mantra whispered through my prayers as my fingers moved delicately through his hair.

With every twist and curl, I invited him to visualize energy radiating from his scalp, washing over him, illuminating his potential. Slowly, his energy began to shift; I could see it in the way his shoulders relaxed and the laughter returned to his eyes. We explored the strength found in authenticity, and after I completed his style, he turned to me, a bright smile adorning his face.

"This is who I am," he said, running his fingers through his curls. "Thank you for helping me see that."

Witnessing these breakthroughs reminds me of the profound responsibility we carry as healers. The act of listening, deeply listening to both words and energy, has become central to my practice. I find that it's not only about the stories shared, but the unspoken energy that dances in the room. There are moments when clients enter my salon with chaotic energy, and my role is to help them attune to a frequency of healing.

Energy exchange is the heartbeat of my salon a river of connection flowing between client and healer. I often liken it to a delicate dance; I read the rhythm of their bodies and adjust to the movement of their spirits. If a client enters anxious or closed off, I focus on gently guiding them toward relaxation. With each soothing word and intentional touch, we create a supportive space where vulnerabilities can be acknowledged and transformed.

Another powerful example is Sarah, who, at first glance, appeared untroubled. But on a deeper level, she harbored insecurities that clouded her light. As I started working on her hair, a simple yet elegant updo I noticed how closely she watched her reflection in the mirror, scrutinizing every detail. This was a telltale sign of her internal struggle, and I felt compelled to connect with her on a more profound level.

"Sarah," I said softly, "I invite you to let go of any self-judgment you may be holding onto. You deserve to be seen and celebrated for who you are."

She hesitated for a moment, the reflection of uncertainty apparent in her eyes. I placed my hand on her shoulder in a gentle gesture of support, emphasizing the energy of love and acceptance. "Let's transform this energy together," I added, my voice imbued with sincerity, as I began to create soft twists and turns in her hair.

Gradually, the tension in her face softened as she looked at her reflection with kinder eyes. I recognized the moment she began to

78

embrace the beauty that lay before her instead of comparing it to an unrealistic standard. As I added delicate hairpins to secure her style, I shared thoughts on the concept of beauty being multidimensional, emphasizing that true radiance shines from within.

By the time we unveiled her finished look, she had undergone a transformation that extended far beyond the physical. Sarah stood before the mirror, her smile breaking open like dawn after a long night. "Kady, I've never felt so beautiful," she said, her voice laced with gratitude. "Thank you for helping me see the truth I was denying."

Each appointment becomes a healing symphony, a manifestation of connection, vulnerability, and empowerment. I understand that my role is not just that of a stylist but also of a vessel through which energy flows, facilitating transformation. It is this understanding that marries my practices of hairdressing and Reiki, nurturing a holistic healing experience.

Listening is by far the most profound lesson I have learned on this journey. I have discovered that the words spoken are often just the surface of what needs to be addressed. A client's energy may reveal more of their story than their lips ever could. By fostering an environment of active listening, I create a space where expression can flourish.

With every client that graces my salon, we embark on a journey of discovery. I prioritize their narratives, weaving them into the personal tapestry of my practice. Moments of healing are not merely serendipitous occurrences but intentionally cultivated exchanges reminders of the powerful process of transformation.

As I close this portion of our journey together, I can't help but reflect on the complexity and beauty of healing during these appointments. Each style I create holds meaning, each exchange resonates on deeper levels, and each fulfilled client represents a milestone in our shared journey.

In my heart, I know that the healing process is never static it continuously evolves as we grow in connection with ourselves and others. I cherish each moment, each client, and each exchange, knowing that within the sacred ritual of hairdressing lies a world of healing, love, and transformation. Together, we are alchemists, transforming our stories, embracing our truths, and celebrating the unique essence that resides in us all.

Client Transformations

Stories of Change

In the bustling heart of Kady's salon, the air was thick with the fusion of laughter, stories, and the familiar hum of hairdryers. Each client brought a piece of their world into this space, creating a mosaic of lives intertwined by the art of hairdressing and the power of healing. As Kady prepared her tools, she often felt like a conductor, orchestrating not just a styling session, but a symphony of transformation and empowerment.

One particularly memorable client, Amira, walked through the door, her heart heavy with the burdens of recent heartbreak. At twenty-eight, she had just gone through a painful separation that left her feeling like a shell of her former self. Amira's thick, curly hair hung limply, a stark contrast to the vibrant spirit Kady had once witnessed radiating from her.

"Hey, dear queen Amira," Kady greeted warmly, hoping to see the familiar spark in her eyes.

"Hi, Kady," Amira replied, her voice barely above a whisper.

As Kady gestured for Amira to take a seat, she noticed her eyes, dull and reflective, scanning the salon's decor. The vibrant colors that surrounded them, the inspirational quotes peppered on the walls, seemed lost on her that day. Kady gently draped a robe over Amira's shoulders, initiating their ritualistic transformation.

"Tell me what's on your mind," Kady prompted, mixing compassion with a gentle professionalism.

"I just…I feel like I've lost myself," Amira confessed, hesitating as tears welled up. "My hair, it feels like a reflection of my heartache. I haven't had the strength to care for it, and now it just feels so… disconnected, like me."

Kady's heart ached for her. She understood how deeply intertwined a person's self-image could be with their hair. She had seen it countless times: hair could symbolize confidence, beauty, and, at times, the weight of emotional burdens.

"Let's change that today," Kady said, her voice taking on a soothing tone. "We're going to breathe some life back into your hair and into you."

As she began to wash Amira's hair, Kady immersed her energy into the water, visualizing it washing away the heaviness that clung to her client like an unwanted shadow. The conversation flowed easily as Kady gently led Amira through the process each strand of hair a pathway to her emotions.

"Tell me about the hair you used to love," Kady encouraged, pouring in her own energy as she massaged Amira's scalp.

Amira's eyes glimmered with nostalgic warmth. "I used to wear it big and wild, and I felt so free! I'd walk into a room and everyone would notice. It was much more than just hair; it was a statement!"

Kady smiled, encouraging Amira to recognize the beauty she had lost sight of. "Let's bring that back. We'll create a style that honors your roots, your strength, and all that you are able to become."

With skilled hands, Kady crafted a bold voluminous curly hairstyle, using the right products to enhance Amira's natural texture. The transformation began not just physically, but also emotionally. As Amira caught glimpses of herself in the mirror, her expression slowly shifted from uncertainty to curiosity and excitement.

When Kady finished, she turned Amira's chair to face the mirror directly. "Take a look."

Amira gasped, her hand instinctively reaching to touch the bouncy curls that now framed her face. "Oh my God, I don't even recognize myself!"

"That's the point," Kady said, her heart swelling with joy. "You are not just your struggles, Amira. You are beautiful, powerful, and deserving of joy."

In that moment, as Amira began to smile for the first time that day, Kady felt a sense of fulfillment that resonated deeply. The release of heavy energy was palpable, and Kady couldn't help but reflect on how every haircut could lead to new beginnings.

Another memorable transformation was with Malik, a young man in his early thirties who had come to Kady following a major career setback. Formerly a rising star in local theater, a sudden health issue had forced him to take time off. When he finally returned to the world, he found himself hesitant, doubting his abilities, and feeling lost.

As Malik settled into the salon chair, he cast a wary glance at Kady through the mirror. "I don't know what I'm doing here, Kady. I've been hiding from the world. Hair is the least of my problems right now."

Kady smiled, undeterred. "Sometimes, it's the smallest changes that can lead to the biggest transformations. Let's start with your hair what's stopping you from feeling like yourself?"

"I used to have this really edgy undercut, and it made me feel confident," he admitted, a tinge of embarrassment creeping into his voice. "But since everything happened, I've let it grow out. Now I just feel... bland."

She could feel Malik's hesitation but knew that a haircut alone wouldn't suffice. "What if we reclaim that edge? What if we give you a style that honors your journey?"

As Kady transformed Malik's hair back into his signature look and installed some instant locs to match his energy, she infused their conversation with empowerment. They discussed the shadows of self-doubt that lingered in the theater community and the power of resilience. Kady shared her own experiences with rejection and doubt, revealing how every setback was a stepping stone to growth.

"I can't believe I'm back to this," Malik said, his voice edged with a mix of disbelief and hope as he observed the whole hair due taking shape.

"You're reclaiming your narrative," Kady reminded him. "This haircut symbolizes your return, your passion a commitment to the art that flows within you."

Once she had sculpted the hair to Malik's satisfaction, Kady spun his chair around to reveal the finished product. The edgy undercut contrasted strikingly against his facial features, reigniting the spark in his eyes.

"I look amazing!" Malik exclaimed, standing as both a physical and emotional metamorphosis. "I actually feel ready to get back on stage."

Kady watched with pride as he marveled at his reflection, feeling invigorated by the possibility that lay ahead. Each transformation reinforced the notion that hair could serve as a powerful reminder of one's identity, resilience, and authenticity.

Then there was Sofia, a recently retired healthcare worker who had devoted decades to serving others. With her change in life's direction came an urgent desire for a complete transformation. The years of wearing her hair in a simple bun had started to feel like a metaphor for her own life bound and restrained.

"I'm here because I want something wild and freeing," Sofia told Kady during the consultation.

Kady empathized; after years of caring for everyone else, it was time for Sofia to focus on herself. "Let's create a look that embodies your newfound freedom, shall we? Tell me, what does wild and free mean to you?"

"I want vibrant colors, something that captures the essence of adventure," Sofia said, her eyes dazzling with excitement.

Kady eagerly agreed to take the plunge with bold hues that spoke to her client's fierce spirit. As she applied the color, vivid tones of purple and teal transformed Sofia's naturally dark hair, each brush stroke infused with energy. Kady explained the color theory behind the shades, emphasizing how each color represented aspects of one's emotions and vitality.

Throughout the process, Sofia shared stories from her childhood her dreams of traveling, the places she wanted to visit, and the vibrant experiences she hoped to embrace. As Kady worked, she not only transformed Sofia's hair but also cultivated a space for self-reflection where her dreams could take flight again.

After rinsing out the dye, Kady began to shape the new hairstyle. Turning Sofia's chair to face the mirror, Kady's heart thudded as she unveiled the transformation.

Sofia gasped. "I feel like…a new person! This is breathtaking. I can't believe I let my hair reflect a life of restraint for so long!"

"The hair reflects your spirit, Sofia. Embrace this change as a celebration of your journey each color a brushstroke of your story," Kady affirmed.

Sofia left the salon that day, radiant and alive. The vibrant colors radiated warmth and joy; they echoed the new chapter unfolding before her, while Kady felt grateful to have facilitated another beautiful transformation grounded in connection, trust, and empowerment.

Each story shared in Kady's salon was a testament to the intricate relationship between physical appearance and emotional health. She witnessed the palpable changes ignite within her clients as they allowed themselves to shed the burdens of the past and embrace the magic of the present.

Then there was Jason, a teenager who walked in with the heaviness of adolescence weighing him down. He had long, unkempt hair that hung in his face, concealing his vibrant personality. Kady quickly learned that Jason had been bullied at school for his uniqueness, leaving him feeling isolated and misunderstood.

As Kady could sense his reluctance to fully engage, she asked gently, "What do you wish for your hair to express?"

"I don't know," he mumbled, hardly making eye contact. "I'm just tired of people making fun of me."

Kady nodded, understanding the significance of self-expression through hair. "I believe your hair can reflect who you truly are inside. Are you ready to let it speak that ?"

Through encouraging dialogue, Kady guided Jason on a transformative journey that would foster self-acceptance. As she washed his hair, she emphasized the cleansing process, speaking to his inner beauty that had been overshadowed by other people's opinions.

"There's so much power in embracing yourself," she whispered, noticing him visibly start to relax. "Let's uncover that!"

Once Jason's hair was clean, Kady opted for soft twist layers that framed his face while maintaining an air of approachability. Together, they chose a few highlights that hinted at the spark of individuality that Jason had kept bottled up for so long.

As Kady worked, the conversation flourished; Jason began to reveal snippets of his hobbies, his love for art, and a passion for creating music. Kady infused their discussions with acceptance and encouragement, reminding him that his identity was to be celebrated.

The moment she revealed the finished look, Kady felt the familiar thrill of witnessing change. Jason stared in amazement at his reflection, a mix of disbelief and joy etched on his features.

"I... I love it!" His voice cracked, overwhelmed with emotion. "I never thought I could look like this. Thank you!"

"You deserve to feel proud of your individuality," Kady beamed, excited for Jason's newfound confidence. "Your hair is now a canvas for your own story."

Jason walked out of the salon that day, standing a little taller, as if he had finally shed the shroud of doubt. Kady watched him leave, knowing that she had ignited a light within him that would shine brightly in the world, echoing a message of self-love and authenticity.

Kady believed deeply in the stories of change that unfolded through her work each client's journey revealed a unique challenge and triumph. These transformations were not just about hair; they were sacred moments of vulnerability, healing, and rebirth.

The emotional depth of each interaction reminded Kady that personal growth would lead to abundance, connection, and joy. With every haircut, she crafted spaces where self-discovery unfolded, urging her clients to embrace their journeys while reclaiming their narratives.

In the end, hairdressing became more than a profession; it emerged as an alchemy of healing and artistry. Kady watched as her clients shed their pasts, overcoming struggles and fears, while they infused their lives with newfound strength and beauty.

As she reflected on the transformations borne from her salon, Kady felt invigorated, grateful to bear witness to the stories of change that inspired her heart and soul. Each client painted a unique tapestry, reminding her that the connection between hair and healing offered profound opportunities for every individual to rise anew.

The Unseen Impact

The vibrant atmosphere of the salon is charged with energy as Kady prepares for another day of transformation. The warm rays of sunlight stream through the large windows, illuminating her well-loved workspace decorated with potted plants, inspiration boards plastered with positive affirmations, and a colorful array of hair products. Each bottle, comb, and tool carries a story of its own, but today, Kady is particularly attuned to the stories of her clients the myriad lives intersecting in her space, each presenting an opportunity for healing and transformation.

As Kady begins her day, she reflects on the manifestations of her work beyond the immediate moment in the salon chair. Each haircut, braids or twist style, and Reiki session is not merely a transaction; it is a thread woven into the larger tapestry of her clients' lives. Over the years, she has witnessed countless transformations, but what truly captivates her is how the energy exchanged in her chair reverberates through her clients' relationships, careers, and self-perception.

One of her favorite stories is about Zara, a young woman who came to Kady during a turbulent time in her life. Zara had recently gone through a difficult breakup and was struggling with her self-image. Her shoulders slumped, and her eyes seemed dull when she first sat down in Kady's chair. As they talked, Kady learned that Zara had always defined herself by her relationships, often neglecting her own dreams in the process. She had dreams of becoming an artist, yet each time she tried to pursue them, self-doubt would creep in, chaining her to her insecurities.

As Kady began to work on Zara's hair, she brought her attention to the act itself a sacred ceremony that involved care, intention, and love. With each snip of the scissors, she infused Zara's hair with positive energy and encouragement. Kady invited Zara to envision who she wanted to be, encouraging her to embrace her identity as an artist. With every creative choice Kady made, Zara began to shed her old skin, allowing Kady's energy to guide a rebirth.

The miraculous moment came when Zara glanced at herself in the mirror. The vibrant color of micro Nubian twist Kady's signature had applied seemed to illuminate not just her hair but the very essence of her spirit. Kady watched as Zara's face transformed from uncertainty to a radiant smile. In that moment, she didn't just see herself differently; she felt renewed . As their time together came to an end, Zara left the salon not only with a stunning new style but with a palpable sense of hope anchored in her heart.

Months later, Kady received a surprise visit from Zara. She walked in with an air of confidence that was unmistakable. "Kady!" she exclaimed, "You won't believe what happened!" Zara revealed that the moment she left the salon, she began to create art again. She had shared her work online, and to her astonishment, it was met with enthusiasm and encouragement from friends and strangers alike. The transformation in her self-perception had given her the courage to embrace her creative identity. With every brushstroke, Zara became more connected to her true self, and in turn, she began to inspire others in her community.

Listening to Zara's story filled Kady with joy and pride. Each time a client shared a transformative experience, it reaffirmed Kady's belief that her work was more than a profession; it was a calling. She understood that the energy exchanged between her and her clients had the power to ripple outward, influencing not only their lives but also the lives of those around them. The bond she established with her clients often transcended the salon, fostering a community of support and affirmation.

Another client, Marcus, had gravitated to Kady's salon after a particularly challenging tenure at work. Uncertain about his career progression, he had become increasingly anxious and self-critical. Kady first met Marcus when he entered the salon with disheveled hair and a heavy heart. As she worked, they engaged in conversation that slowly ebbed the tension from his shoulders. With gentle guidance, Kady helped him articulate his dreams and aspirations, and as she shaped his hair, he found his words gaining clarity.

As Kady shared stories about her own journey, Marcus was inspired to confront his fears. "I've always wanted to start my own business," he confessed one day, his voice trembling with newfound vulnerability. "But I just don't know if I'm cut out for it." Kady's response was simple yet profound: "What if you are? What if you let your passion guide you?"

Kady encouraged Marcus to lean into his creativity and establish a vision for his business. The renewed sense of energy coursing through him was evident in his vibrant new haircut. Armed with confidence, Marcus took steps toward entrepreneurship, weaving the lessons he learned in Kady's chair into his professional life.

As weeks turned into months, Kady watched as Marcus's business blossomed, becoming a hub for creative collaboration in their community. His journey became an embodiment of resilience and innovation, and Kady felt privileged to have shared that formative experience with him. It wasn't just about great hair; it was about nurturing dreams and aspirations that carried a more profound communal significance.

Through these narrative threads of transformation, Kady began to recognize a common thread among her clients an unseen impact that often continued long after they walked out of her salon. She learned that the energy exchanged in the salon chair had a catalytic effect, instilling hope, courage, and self-acceptance. Alongside this, Kady found herself embracing the role of a guide and witness, solidifying the importance of vulnerability and honesty in her practice.

One day, as she closed up the salon, Kady received a text from another client, Nina, who had recently completed her first art show a project that seemed unimaginable just a year before. They had worked together on Nina's self-image, diving into deep personal reflections and extensive dream mapping during their appointments. As Nina's journey unfolded, Kady observed her embracing her identity with grace and affirmation.

Nina wrote about the encouragement she received, stating, "Your belief in me meant everything, Kady. Thank you for holding space during a time when I felt like I was fading away." Kady felt a rush of warmth flood her chest. She understood that the beauty of her work was not quantifiable; it was woven into the fabric of the community around her.

Kady realized that the true measure of her success was not in the number of clients or the cut and colors completed but rather in the empowerment she instilled in each individual who sat in her chair.

The chains of transformation had a way of creating connections between clients, many of whom were now actively supporting one another. Kady began organizing community events at the salon where clients could gather not just to celebrate their transformations but also to uplift each other. These events fostered a sense of belonging, inviting conversations that nurtured each person's journey.

At a recent gathering, Kady overheard Zara and Marcus sharing their various journeys the triumphs, the stumbles, the lessons learned. The air was electric with positivity. It was extraordinary to witness

92

the organic rapport fostering a collective transformation among her clients. Connections formed organically, and Kady reveled in a newfound understanding: the invisible web created through her work was a community of empowerment, challenging one another to dream bigger and reach higher.

As she reflected on all of this, Kady felt a stirring within her to expand her impact further into the community. She envisioned workshops that would allow clients to share their stories and skills, empowering them collectively. She imagined art classes led by Zara or small business discussions hosted by Marcus. Through collaboration, they could create synergies that nurtured creativity, confidence, and support.

Kady picked up her journal, eager to outline her vision for these workshops. As she penned her aspirations, she felt a surge of inspiration. Her work was more than hairdressing and Reiki healing; it was a conduit for community building. Kady recognized that each interaction was a vital ingredient in creating an alchemical process: a synthesis of healing artistry interwoven with the energetic tapestry of each individual's life.

In the months that followed, Kady organized various events that transformed her salon into a sanctuary of creativity and collaboration. Community leaders, artists, and entrepreneurs shared their insights with enthusiastic attendees who had once felt isolated in their struggles. Zara painted live, inspiring others to share their art, while Marcus led discussions on business development and motivation.

Kady stepped back and observed the vibrant interactions. She smiled as she watched her clients connect and uplift each other former strangers now nurturing a community grounded in healing and support. Each person who entered her salon brought their unique stories; together, they formed a colorful mosaic underscored by trust, compassion, and collective transformation.

The conversations echoed within the walls of her sanctuary stories of growth, resilience, and healing. With each gathering, Kady noticed a deepened sense of pride in her work. She realized that through her passion, she was not only facilitating individual healing journeys but also nurturing a resilient community that thrived on connection.

It was particularly touching to hear testimonials from clients who openly shared how Kady's influence had intertwined with their lives. Zara spoke about her newfound confidence that allowed her to connect deeply within her art community. Marcus shared how his business had become a platform for advocacy, encouraging others to chase their passions. Nina's art show not only celebrated her journey but had opened doors to collaborations with local organizations dedicated to supporting emerging artists.

As Kady stood in the midst of her community, the emotional current pulsed around her a beautiful reminder that her work had catalyzed transformations that reached far beyond the salon. Kady recognized that her role extended beyond a traditional stylist; she had become a nurturer of dreams, a holder of space, and a healer of both individuals and the community.

The unseen impact of her work flourished with every interaction and ripple effect, reinforcing her mission of empowerment and connection. Kady's heart swelled with gratitude as she silently acknowledged the web of healing she had co-created, bringing together diverse stories of transformation, growth, and collective support.

As the gathering wound down, Kady looked around at the faces illuminated with hope and connection. Each story was a testament to the power of healing, validation, and love all cultivated in a space that began with hair, but grew to encompass so much more. It was a sacred journey that promised to continue blooming, evolving, and enriching lives in ways that Kady could only begin to fathom.

In that moment, she knew that this was only the beginning, and she felt profoundly connected to the journey ahead a journey where the unseen impact of her work would ripple into infinity, creating expansive transformations in her community for years to come.

Client Testimonials

As I sit quietly in the warm, inviting sanctuary of my salon, I reflect on the myriad voices that have passed through my chair. Each client brings a unique story, a tapestry of experiences woven together by their journeys of self-discovery and transformation. The healing power of hairdressing transcends mere aesthetics; it is a sacred bond that can profoundly impact both stylist and client. Today, I want to share a few powerful testimonials that encapsulate the essence of this connection, allowing the voices of my clients to resonate with you as deeply as they have with me.

"Testimonial: A 12-Year Journey of Haircare, Healing, and Sisterhood

I've been going to Kady Beauty for 12 years, and I can honestly say it's been one of the greatest blessings God has ever placed in my life. When I first came to Kady, I was overwhelmed, frustrated with my natural hair, and didn't want to return to chemical relaxers—but I also wasn't doing well managing it on my own. I was hesitant about getting braids, uncertain about the process, and worried about my hairline thinning like I'd seen happen to so many women.

Kady not only reassured me, but she also educated me. She explained what causes hairline damage and showed me how to protect my edges, even while wearing braids. Twelve years later, my hairline is still healthy, and my edges are intact. That alone is a testimony to her skill, care, and integrity.

Back then, I was still coloring my grays, trying to hold on to a look

I thought I had to maintain. As time passed and more silver strands appeared, I felt led to embrace my natural hair color—and Kady supported me every step of the way. She transitioned the colors of my braids to blend beautifully with my grays, and today, at 56, I receive constant compliments on how elegant and seamless my hair looks. She even encourages me to experiment with color in ways that are both tasteful and true to my personality. My style is professional, timeless, and a little edgy—and Kady captures that perfectly every time.

As a business owner working in professional spaces, my appearance matters. But with Kady, my hair is one less thing I ever have to worry about. She understands the importance of looking polished and poised, and she delivers that with excellence every time.

But more than a hairstylist, Kady has become family. Over the years, we've prayed for each other, encouraged one another, and walked through life's ups and downs together. I've watched her children grow into wonderful young adults, and she has done the same for my family. My daughter started getting her hair done by Kady as a child, and now, as a grown woman, she continues to go to her. Even my mother has been in Kady's chair, and Kady's gentleness and expertise met their unique needs with compassion.

I had prayed for someone who truly knew how to care for hair—a professional with integrity and a heart aligned with God. What I received was far more: a woman of God who honors her gift, treats people with love, and brings peace into every appointment.

"After 12 years, I can honestly say I don't trust anyone else to do my hair. Kady is more than a stylist. She is anointed for this work. God placed her in my life at just the right time, and through her hands, I've not only maintained healthy hair—I've found rest, friendship, and sisterhood."

— **Angela, Texas**

"I walked into Kady's salon feeling like a shadow of myself. I had just gone through a tough breakup that left me questioning my worth. My hair was a mess; I hadn't styled it properly in weeks. Kady sat me down, looked me in the eye, and told me that I was beautiful. She took the time to listen to my story, and as she worked her magic, I felt the layers of my sadness and self-doubt begin to peel away. When she finished, I hardly recognized myself not just because of my new style, but because I started to see the person I could be again. Kady didn't just do my hair; she resurrected my spirit." Elina, 28

Elina's courage to share her story with me affected me profoundly. In her experience, I recognized themes of vulnerability and renewal that mirrored my own journey. It reminded me that each haircut is not merely a physical transformation but also an emotional release. It is a chance for clients to reclaim their power after difficult moments in their lives. Elina became not only a client but a part of my community, and in her healing, I, too, found the strength to reflect on my role as a vessel for transformation.

"My daughter and I had a tradition of going to get her hair styled before every school year, but the summer before seventh grade, I couldn't afford it. My heart sank as I watched her disappointment. When I linked up with Kady to talk about a collaboration, she insisted on doing my daughter's hair for free. I was in tears as I watched Kady braid and twist with such love. She involved my daughter in the process and empowered her by teaching her about the beauty of her own hair. My daughter walked out with a hairstyle that gave her confidence on her first day back at school, but more importantly, the smile on her face was a reminder that kindness can change lives. Kady helped us both realize that beauty comes from within." Mariama, 37

Mariama's story resonates with the essence of my work community spirit. It wouldn't have mattered how intricate the hairstyle was if it didn't embody the love and connection shared between them that day. Through this personal moment, I understood the importance of passing on traditions, love, and confidence to the next generation. It reminded me that each client I serve carries the responsibility to uplift those around them, often unconsciously redefining the narrative of what beauty means in their lives.

"I had never heard of Reiki before my first appointment with Kady. When she mentioned incorporating energy work into my hair session, I was a bit skeptical, but I was open-minded. That day, I felt as if I was receiving a warm hug from the universe. Kady's hands felt like they were filled with love and understanding. As she combed through my hair, I felt old wounds being healed. Each stroke of the comb felt like a release. By the end of the appointment, I had not only a gorgeous transformation, a vibrant color that felt true to who I am but also a sense of calm I hadn't felt in years. I couldn't believe that a haircut could provoke such profound feelings!" Amina, 31

Amina's testimonial illuminated for me the seamless fusion of hairdressing and Reiki. She reminded me how vital it is to extend the practice of healing beyond the physical into the emotional and spiritual realms. Amina's journey with me became a sacred space for her to explore and release her past burdens through simple yet profound transformative practices. Her experience validated my belief that when we nurture ourselves, we are also nurturing our connection to the world, heightening our ability to empathize and uplift others.

"The moment I met Kady, I felt an instant connection. I had been struggling with alopecia for years, and my self-esteem was at an all time low. She welcomed me with open arms and an open heart. As we talked about my hair, she encouraged me to embrace my uniqueness. She specifically tailored her signature micro Nubian twist just for me, lightweight and Gorgeous. The first time she styled my hair, it was the first time I felt beautiful in a long time. Kady worked with me to celebrate my hair loss instead of hiding it. She helped me experiment with glamorous pieces and gave me the strength to showcase who I truly am. I no longer hide behind my hair; I wear it like a crown." Jamila, 25

Jamila's story beautifully embodies the depth of self-acceptance. Her journey reminds me that, as a stylist, my responsibility transcends making hair look beautiful. It is about igniting that spark of confidence that allows clients like her to feel empowered in their identities. In the face of adversity and societal pressure, I saw her transformation unfold, affirming my commitment to nurturing beauty in all its forms, even in absence. It is in these vulnerable exchanges that I learned that true beauty blossoms from acceptance and love, the core pillars of effective healing.

"I had to learn to love myself, flaws and all. After my appointment with Kady, I left her salon feeling reborn. My hair had never looked better, but it was more than just the hairstyle that uplifted me. It was Kady, her energy, her ability to listen and understand my struggles. We spoke about body positivity, self-love, and what it truly means to be beautiful from the inside out. I never thought I would connect with someone while sitting in a salon chair. Kady opened my eyes to the power of my own narrative and encouraged me to own my story passionately. I walked out a new person with a renewed sense of purpose and love for myself." Sophie, 29

In Sophie's reflection, I felt the weight of our conversations resonate with my purpose a synergy of artistry and healing. Our discussions touched on the underlying beliefs we carry about beauty, often influenced by society's perceptions. It became clear to me how significant our exchanges are; the chair transforms into a space of revelation and reclamation. Witnessing Sophie embrace her flaws as beautiful treasures invigorated my resolve to cultivate a space for open dialogue and support.

"My experience with Kady was unlike any other. Honestly, I came in just wanting a haircut, but what I received was a holistic overhaul of my mindset. I had been feeling lost and stagnant in my career and personal life. While Kady worked on my hair, her soothing words guided me through reflection. She asked the right questions, which led to deep insights. I felt re energized not just because of my new look but because Kady illuminated possibilities I had never considered. I left the salon ready to embrace change in every area of my life." David, 40

David's transformation underscored the idea that true change often begins with a willingness to confront one's self-limiting beliefs. His brave foray into discussing career stagnation in a salon chair reinforced the importance of vulnerability during transformational moments. I felt humbled that our session had served as his launching pad into a new chapter of life. For me, this confirmed that the dialogue we share extends beyond beauty; it is a canvas for growth and inspiration.

As I weave these stories within the tapestry of my practice, I remind myself how intrinsic connection is to my work. Each testimonial not only captures the essence of healing through hairdressing; it serves as a reminder of the responsibility I carry as an artist and healer. These transformations reflect the resonance of mutual empowerment. I often remind my clients that while their stories emerge through the witness of my work, I am equally transformed by the gifts they share with me.

"Before my first appointment, I was feeling low, like my spark had diminished. I was stuck in a rut, feeling invisible in my own life. Kady not only gave me an incredible hairstyle but a deep connection. The moment I sat in her chair, it felt like she wasn' t just doing my hair; she was almost reading my soul. During our session, I could feel my energy shift and my vibrancy return. When I left, I felt unstoppable. Kady taught me that hair is more than just strands; it's an expression of identity! I feel proud to wear my hair the way I want it, not just to fit in." Nina, 33

Nina's journey encapsulated the very spirit of personal agency that I aspire to instill in every client who walks through my door. Her realization that hair is an expression of self feeds the core philosophy that guides my practice. I believe that reclaiming and expressing one's identity is crucial in the healing process. It made me appreciate the trust my clients place in me to facilitate that journey.

"I always thought I was just going in for a trim, but I came out with so much more. Kady turned my mundane hair appointment into a soulful experience. I had no idea how much I needed to hear her words of affirmation. She helped me reconnect with myself during a time of loss. I had lost my mother not long before our session, and Kady helped me honor her legacy by weaving her spirit into my hairstyle. It was more than just a haircut; it was a tribute to love. Kady has a gift for helping others honor their moments." Leonie, 45

Leonie's powerful testimony reaffirmed that our work often honors not only individual journeys but also collective narratives. Her loss highlighted the significance of weaving memory into our transformations. I found immense beauty in her ability to incorporate her grief into a celebration of life, shedding light on how love can manifest through the act of caring for oneself. In this way, hairdressing morphed into a ritual of remembrance and joy.

Client Testimonial

Paula — Temple, Texas

"Let me start by saying that my hair has always been a lifelong challenge. It's naturally fine, very soft, and curly making it difficult to manage and even harder for most beauticians to work with. Over time, it also began to thin, adding to the complexity.

A few years ago, feeling overwhelmed and unsure of what to do, I turned to prayer. I asked God to guide me to someone who could not only understand my hair but also help me embrace it just as it is.

I searched online and came across Kady. Before booking the appointment, I prayed once more—asking for clarity and confirmation that she was the right one.

From the moment I met her, I knew.

At my very first visit, she examined my hair with care and helped me choose a style tailored to its unique texture and needs. In time, I began to feel called to start a loc journey—but I hesitated, unsure if it was even possible with my hair's condition.

Kady reminded me gently:

"With God, all things are possible."

She encouraged me to trust the process.

Now, three years later, my hair is beautifully locked and I couldn't be happier."

Paula, Texas.

"I started with Mrs. Kady almost a year ago, after accidentally doing the BIG CHOP—lol! My hair was short and shaved on the sides, and I wasn't sure what could be done. But Kady worked her magic with the micro Nubian twists and, to my surprise, she was even able to braid the shaved parts. Those twists took ten years off my face! My friends and family were amazed.

Kady didn't just style my hair—she prayed with me and touched and agreed with me for growth. And now, a year later, I'm preparing to transition into the real thing: locs. Her micro twists were the perfect substitute for a loc'd look without the commitment. Now I'm ready for the full journey.

Kady is sweet, gifted, and truly lovely. I recommend her to anyone who asks about my hair. I love her. You're in the best hands ever."

Martha, Satisfied Client.

"Kadybeauty Seer, here is my written testimonial.

Client Name: Rene Wilson

Testimonial: I'd had the pleasure of knowing Ms. Kady for over two years now, and I can confidently say she is one of the most talented and professional braiders I've ever met.

Since entrusting Kadybeauty with my hair, I've noticed significant growth and improvement in its overall health. Not only do her styles protect and nurture my hair, but they also turn heads. I've received countless compliments on how beautiful and unique my braids look.

Ms. Kady's skill, attention to detail, and warm personality, peaceful environment make every appointment a joy! I'm so grateful my coworker recommended me to her!"

Rene Wilson, Texas.

"Good morning Khadi,

I must take a moment to express my deepest gratitude for Kadybeauty Seer, who has been transforming my hair and my daughter's hair since 2018. Kady is more than just a talented braider; she possesses a unique understanding of the spiritual connection we have with our hair. Each time we sit in her chair, we are not just receiving a hairstyle, but an experience that honors our beauty and individuality.

Kady's work is truly magical. She listens and connects with us, ensuring we leave her salon not only looking our best but also feeling uplifted and empowered. Her passion and dedication shine through in every braid, making each visit a celebration of our hair and spirit. I cannot recommend her enough—she never disappoints!

Thank you, Kady, for your incredible artistry and for nurturing the bond between us and our hair. You are a true gift from God!"

Monique Capri: Author, Neuron coding Coach, Minister in

104

training and student Acupuncturist.

Every client's narrative enriches my understanding of the diverse experiences that shape our lives. They remind me that we are all part of a greater tapestry, interconnected in our journeys and supportive of one another's progress. This chapter highlights how the work we do in the salon extends beyond hair; it is about creating a safe space where clients can uncover their strengths, process their emotions, and embrace new beginnings.

As I reflect on the power of these testimonials, I'm reminded of my own growth as a healer and stylist. It is a reciprocal dance of energy, where gratitude and transformation flow back and forth. I cultivate an environment where both clients and I can explore new dimensions of beauty, healing, and connection. Each service becomes a sacred ritual an alchemy that ties our experiences together, intertwining the art of hairdressing with the depths of spiritual healing.

In this journey, I embrace the revelations shared by my clients, their stories echoing through the strands of hair we tend to in our moments together. We are reminded that healing does not exist in isolation; it thrives within community, connection, and vulnerability. Let us continue to uplift one another as we embrace every transformation, weaving a future rich with possibility and light.

Energy Alignment and Attraction

The Power of Alignment

Energy alignment is a concept that runs deep within the veins of both my personal journey and professional practice. As I reflect on the years I've invested in hairdressing and the healing art of Reiki, I see that the underlying theme connecting them is the extraordinary power of alignment. It's about tuning into oneself, understanding desires, and realizing that the universe responds vibrantly when we harmonize our energies with intention.

When I first began my hairdressing career, I treated each appointment solely as a technical challenge. I meticulously mirrored my tools against the strands of hair before me, focused solely on perfection whether it was layering, balayage , or the perfect curl. However, over time, I discovered that the true artistry wasn't just in technique, but also in energy.

I vividly recall my early days in the salon. I had a regular client, Maria, who wasn't just a client; she became a pivotal character in my own story of alignment. Every time Maria scheduled an appointment, I would feel an air of excitement coupled with a tinge of anxiety. She was going through a tumultuous phase in her life, seeking transformation not only in her hairstyle but also in her heart.

In our initial sessions, Maria would share her struggles with self-esteem. With each cut, she released not just hair, but the weight of her worries. I realized then that the energy circulating between us her vulnerability and my focus created a sacred space that welcomed alignment. I began to understand the importance of being aware of both my energy and that of my clients. When I was fully present, I noticed a shift in my work; the styles I crafted were more vibrant, and the reactions from clients became more profound.

During one particularly memorable appointment, Maria shared her aspiration to start her own business. She feared that she would struggle to achieve her dreams. I paused, scissors in hand, reflecting deeply on her words. I encouraged her to embrace the energy of her aspirations. "What if," I began, "you approached your goals as if they were already within reach? Envision your success as a reality you're stepping into rather than merely dreaming of." As she processed my words, I could see the spark reignite in her eyes, and the contours of her face softened as she began to align with her desires.

As I worked on her hair, I envisioned her vision her new business flourishing, her confidence radiating. I infused Reiki energy into my movements, drawing from the well of positive energy and vibrant intentions that flowed through me in that moment. When I finally showed her the mirror, the joy that lit her face was not merely about the hairstyle; it was about stepping into an aligned version of herself. This moment underscored for me that alignment is a potent force in the healing process.

Another beautiful example of alignment emerged with my client Jameela. She entered my salon overwhelmed, her hair requiring a transformation that mirrored her personal struggle in life. As she settled down in my chair, I sensed the resistance she carried. I took a deep breath, grounding myself in the awareness that her journey was not solely physical but also deeply emotional.

"Jameela," I said gently, "Let's set an intention for this appointment. What do you wish to walk away with today?" She hesitated, unsure. I encouraged her to think of this as an invitation to align with her truth. Together, we whispered her intentions into the air: resilience, confidence, and renewal.

With each clip and stroke of the brush, I focused intently on channeling that energy into her hair. The atmosphere Shifted; what began as uncertainty blossomed into possibilities. As we finished her transformation, Jameela looked in the mirror, visibly lighter. "I feel different," she whispered, as if voicing a new awakening.

Seeing these changes unfold around me was transformative in itself. It became evident to me that success wasn't measured only in the physical appearance of my clients but in their emotional growth and self-realization. The alignment of energies during these interactions led to outcomes that were far greater than I could have known as a hairdresser.

As I delved further into this concept of energy alignment, I began to understand the profound significance of self-awareness in manifesting desires. In my practice, the law of attraction serves as a catalyst, but without alignment, the desire remains stagnant an unplanted seed.

Journaling became an essential tool for this process. I dedicated mornings to reflecting on my thoughts and energy levels, creating a space to identify where I felt aligned and where there were blockages. There were days when I felt vibrant and energized, and others when self-doubt crept in, clouding my vision and intentions. By witnessing these fluctuations, I learned that alignment isn't a destination, but rather a dynamic journey requiring continuous nurturing of the self.

I encourage you to explore this within your own life. Whenever you face challenges, take a moment to reflect on your energy. Are you aligned with your desires, or have you drifted off course? For instance, during a challenging period in my business, I noticed the surge of negative energy manifesting around me client cancellations, miscommunications, and a general heaviness in the salon atmosphere. I had become disconnected from my purpose; my intentions were clouded by external pressures.

It wasn't until I took a step back and re-centered myself that the tide began to shift. I spent days recalibrating, diving into mindfulness practices and affirmations that resonated with my core belief in abundance. Upon returning to the salon with renewed intention, I consciously projected that energy into my encounters with clients. The environment felt lighter. Clients arrived with fresh excitement, unabashedly sharing their aspirations, and the energy of possibility pervaded the space. This taught me firsthand that alignment is an invitation to reclaim your purpose repeatedly to acknowledge when you've veered off path and lovingly guide yourself back.

Our journeys towards alignment often intertwine with self-limiting beliefs. It takes that courageous step of looking inward, confronting our fears, and transmuting them into love. I remember a pivotal experience with a young client named Amina, who felt lost in a world filled with expectations. She stepped into my salon with a heavy heart, believing she was constrained by societal norms. As we discussed hair transformations, she hesitated, battling her desire to express her individuality.

I invited Amina to envision the woman she truly aspired to be radiant, unapologetic, and free. Together, we anchored her aspirations through the styling process. I reflected on my own experiences of placing boundaries, liberating myself from the confines of others' expectations. The energy shifted palpably within our exchange; Amina ultimately chose a bold color that resonated with her radical self-acceptance. Embracing her individuality was not merely about hair color; it embodied a declaration of her identity.

Through these anecdotes, the concept of energy alignment becomes more than a theoretical discussion it morphs into a practical guide for everyday life. It celebrates the beautiful dance between intention, self-awareness, and manifestation. As I reconcile my own experiences, I urge readers to reflect on their alignment: Is there a vibration in your life that feels misaligned? Are there desires shimmering within you that long for attention?

Alignment requires continuous effort and attention. I have woven it into the fabric of my daily practices, surrendering to moments of self-reflection through meditation and grounding techniques learned from my Reiki training. Every morning, I begin with gratitude, expressing thanks for my craft, my clients, and the energetic exchanges we share.

Self-awareness cultivates a richer understanding of the energies we emanate. As I gaze into the mirror each day, I affirm my connection to the world around me and appreciate the power that lies not only within me but also in the symbiotic dance of energies shared with others. When I approach my clients, I strive to create a clear channel for their self-exploration a mirror reflecting not just their physical appearance but the essence of who they are striving to become.

Consider a practice that resonates for you. It could be something simple, such as a daily mantra that captures the core of your intentions. Each time you utter those words, align yourself with the energy they're meant to embody. Notice how your external world mirrors your inner state. Do clients respond with enthusiasm during appointments? Do opportunities arise organically, echoing the energy you've put forth?

Frequently, I encourage my clients to set intentions before a transformation. We close our eyes and share what feels most important to them. These moments become pivotal in fostering alignment, ensuring our energies are in sync. It's during my interactions with clients like Maria and Jameela that I've come to appreciate the latent potential of this practice. What if you pursued engagement with the world, rooted in a clear understanding of your motivations and desires?

The beauty of alignment lies in its intoxicating ripple effect. As I align, I begin to attract clients whose energies resonate with mine. So often, we drift through life seeking validation in external achievements, but in truth, the focus should be inward. When I embrace my light, nurturing my passion as both a hairdresser and healer, I create a space that magnetizes others who are also on their path of self-exploration.

If you're seeking to attract abundance be it in your career, relationships, or personal fulfillment the first step is to root yourself in alignment. Start small; understand what it means to you to be aligned. Write down what you desire. Visualize those aspirations in vivid detail. Envision the feelings associated with your achievements: joy, fulfillment, connection. Allow that energy to fill you.

Alignment also teaches the value of vulnerability. It's okay to acknowledge doubts and moments of misalignment; these experiences are essential to growth. In every appointment, I embrace the imperfection, recognizing it as an opportunity for deeper connection and understanding. I invite my clients to share their struggles, understanding that nurturing our energies often involves confronting fears. Together, we traverse the spectrum of vulnerability, where healing truly begins.

As I share these reflections, I hope to highlight that energy alignment is an ever-evolving journey filled with lessons, opportunities, and the beauty of connection. May these practices inspire you to explore the alignment of your energy, guiding you towards abundant manifestations. The dance of alignment doesn't merely end as we achieve our desires; it is a continuum, constantly leading to new aspirations, new desires, and ultimately, a fuller expression of ourselves.

In the end, manifestation is less about force and more about flows an allowance for the universe to conspire on our behalf when we release the blockages we create. My hairdressing practice amplified through energy alignment serves as a testament to the synchronicity possible when we align intention, energy, and action.

As you embark on your own journey of alignment, remember that the essence of manifestation lies within you. Trust in the process, nurture your energies, and allow abundance to unfold gracefully. Embrace the beautiful tapestry of your journey, and witness the transformation that unfolds as you come into alignment with yourself.

Practical Techniques

In the journey of self-discovery and empowerment, aligning your energy is a crucial step towards attracting the abundance you desire in life. As I guide clients through both hairdressing and Reiki practices, I have found that the techniques of energy alignment can be transformative, helping individuals to harness their power fully. In this subchapter, I will walk you through several practical techniques to help you align your energy effectively.

The path to energy alignment begins with awareness. To create positive change, one must first recognize and understand their current energetic state. Take a moment to pause and assess how you feel in this very moment physically, emotionally, and spiritually. This practice of self-assessment establishes the foundation for all the techniques we will explore.

Our first technique is visualization, a powerful method that engages the mind's eye and activates the energy within. Visualization can take many forms, but it generally involves picturing your desired outcome and feeling that experience as if it is already happening.

To practice visualization, find a quiet space where you can relax without interruptions. Close your eyes and take several deep breaths, inhaling deeply through your nose and exhaling gently through your mouth. With each breath, feel your body relax and your mind clear.

Now, picture a vibrant light at the center of your being. This light represents your energy bright, pure, and full of potential. As you visualize this light, imagine it expanding with each breath you take.

Allow this energy to fill your entire body, radiating warmth and positivity.

Next, envision a specific goal or desire you wish to attract. It could be anything from improved self-confidence to financial abundance or emotional healing. As you picture this outcome, see yourself living it fully. What does it feel like? What thoughts accompany this experience? Who is around you? Engage all your senses what do you hear, smell, or see?

As you visualize, let the feelings of joy, gratitude, and fulfillment flow through you. Believe in your ability to attract this reality, and hold onto that emotion as you finish your visualization. Slowly bring your awareness back to the present moment, and when you're ready, open your eyes.

Incorporating affirmations into your daily routine is another effective technique for aligning your energy. Affirmations are positive statements that help reprogram your subconscious mind, reinforce self-belief, and shift energy toward desired outcomes.

To create your affirmations, consider what you genuinely want to attract in your life. Write down a few statements in the present tense as if you are already experiencing these desires. For example, instead of saying, "I want to feel confident," phrase it as "I am confident and secure in myself." The power of affirmations lies in their ability to reframe your thoughts and emotions.

Once you have created your affirmations, set aside a few moments each day to recite them. You might find it effective to say them aloud in front of a mirror while maintaining eye contact with yourself. This practice creates a deeper connection with your statements and reinforces their significance.

Another interesting way to integrate affirmations is by writing them down. Consider maintaining a dedicated journal where you can craft a list of daily affirmations. Each morning, take a few moments to read and reflect on your affirmations, allowing the words to penetrate your consciousness. Over time, you'll begin to notice a shift in your energy and a stronger alignment with your goals.

Mindfulness practices are essential for maintaining energetic balance and fostering a connection between body, mind, and spirit. Mindfulness encourages living in the present moment with full awareness, allowing you to observe your thoughts and feelings without judgment. This practice cultivates a greater understanding of your energy patterns and helps release what no longer serves you.

To practice mindfulness, start with a simple breathing meditation. Find a comfortable, quiet space to sit or lie down. Close your eyes and take a deep breath in, filling your lungs completely. Hold it for a moment, and then slowly exhale all the air. Repeat this process for a few minutes, focusing solely on your breath.

As thoughts arise, acknowledge them without resistance and gently guide your awareness back to your breath. This practice teaches you to observe your thoughts, regain focus, and let go of distractions that can disrupt your energy alignment.

You may also explore mindfulness in your daily activities. Whether you're washing dishes, walking in nature, or styling hair, practice being fully present. Notice the sensations in your body, the sounds around you, and the visual details of your surroundings. Engaging fully with the moment helps you maintain a heightened sense of awareness and connection to your energy flow.

While each of these techniques stands alone, they also complement one another beautifully. For instance, combining visualization with affirmations can supercharge your energetic alignment. Picture your desired outcome as you confidently affirm your abilities to attract that reality. The synergy between these techniques amplifies their effects, connecting your mind and energy in cohesive harmony.

As an extension of this interconnectedness, let's explore how these techniques relate to the art of hairdressing. Every hairstyle has an energy it carries the vibrational signature of the hairstylist's intention and the client's energy. When I am working with a client, I can feel their energy to some extent. This sense-awareness is similar to mindfulness in both practices, we tune into the present moment and acknowledge the energetic atmosphere.

When I visualize the outcome of a haircut or style, I tap into the essence that hairstyle will capture for the client. I align my creative energy with their unique identity, using visualization to foresee how the result can empower them. This process often transforms both my energy and that of my clients, as we co-create an experience that resonates deeply on a fundamental level.

Additionally, affirmations play a significant role in my practice. As I engage in conversation with clients, I often incorporate affirming words to uplift and empower them. Phrases like "Your beauty shines through your personality" or "Your hair reflects your inner strength" encourage clients to embrace their individuality and align their self-perception with their desired image.

As we engage in this energetic dance during hair appointments, it's fascinating to observe how the combination of energy work and hairdressing enhances the healing process. Just as one can apply the techniques discussed here in a broader context, they can also be seamlessly woven into the practice of hairdressing, creating an environment that fosters energy alignment and transformation.

To help you on your path toward energy alignment and attraction, I encourage you to integrate these practices into your daily routine. Try setting a daily intention where you dedicate time to visualization, affirmations, and mindfulness. Choose one technique to focus on for the week, gradually incorporating others as you grow more comfortable.

Whenever you feel disconnected or misaligned, pause and turn to these practical techniques. Remember that aligning your energy is not merely a destination it is an ongoing journey that requires tending to your energetic garden. Just as I help clients tend to their hair, cultivation and nurturing of our energies require consistent attention and care.

Acknowledge that every day is an opportunity for growth. Allow yourself the grace to embrace this continuous cycle of learning, experimenting, and refining your approach to energy alignment. I encourage you to celebrate your progress, whether it comes through a harmonious sense of balance or a newfound understanding of your energetic patterns.

As I conclude this section, keep in mind that you are the architect of your energy and the creator of your reality. By embracing these practical techniques, you will not only facilitate a more profound connection to yourself but also attract the abundance and vibrancy that life has to offer. Align your energy, and the universe will respond in kind, reflecting your intentions and desires in beautiful ways.

Cultivating Positive Intentions

In the intricate tapestry of our lives, the threads of intention weave the patterns of our experiences. As a healer and hairdresser, I have come to understand that the energy we send out into the world is a reflection of our inner state. This realization has been a pivotal element in my journey, particularly in cultivating positive intentions that resonate with the vibrations I wish to attract.

One of the earliest memories I have of launching intentions occurred during one of my calming rituals before appointments. I would sit on my mat, close my eyes, and visualize the energy I wanted to share with a client. In those moments, I would articulate my intentions clearly: to empower, to uplift, and to inspire joy. As I sat in quiet contemplation, feeling my breath ebb and flow, I understood how profoundly our intentions shape the reality we experience.

One time, I had a client named Sade who was recovering from a difficult breakup. When she first came to me, her energy was heavy, filled with doubt and sadness. She walked into my salon wrapped in a thick coat, seemingly shielding herself from the world. I sensed her hesitation. She was not just there for a haircut; she was looking for a lifeline to reconnect with her sense of self-worth. I set my intention to help her find that spark of joy that had dimmed in her life.

As I combed through her hair, I shared stories about my own experiences of loss and the empowering realizations I had drawn from them. In those shared moments, our energies began to intertwine. I could feel the heaviness in her heart starting to lift, rooted in the connection we were building. During that appointment, she asked me how I maintained such a positive outlook despite life's challenges. I explained that cultivating positive intentions was my guiding light.

"Every morning, I wake up and set my intentions for the day," I told her. "I like to visualize what I want to attract. Some days are harder than others, but I make a conscious choice to invite positivity into my life." As I spoke, I noticed her shoulders relax, her body language opening up. Sade was hungry for that energy, and at that moment, she felt empowered to embrace her journey toward healing.

This experience solidified for me the idea that our intentions can serve as powerful catalysts for transformation. It reminded me of how often I faced challenges in maintaining a positive mindset. There were momentous days when doubt whispered harsh critiques, clouding my vision. In those times, I would reflect on the promises I made to myself about resilience. I discovered that embracing positivity wasn't about ignoring struggles; it was about acknowledging them and choosing to rise above.

In a world filled with distractions and negativity, it's easy to be pulled into a spiral of despair. For me, the remedy became a practice of mindfulness, a conscious effort to redirect my thoughts toward what I wanted rather than what I feared. I began to find solace in journaling, where I could filter through tangled emotions and focus on my intentions. I'd sit with my journal each evening, reflecting on the day's events. What challenges did I face? What opportunities arose? Most importantly, how did I want to perceive these experiences as I moved forward?

Journaling allowed me to check in with my intentions regularly. One night, after a particularly trying week, I poured my heart out on the pages. I wrote about my frustrations and fears but, as I summarized my thoughts, I transformed the narrative into an affirmation of what I wanted to attract: confidence, growth, and supportive connections. I scripted my intentions as if they were already manifest, infusing my words with the energy of possibility. "I am confident and capable," I wrote. "I attract positivity and abundance into my life."

As I read my affirmations back to myself, the act of listening became just as powerful as writing. Those affirmations ignited a sense of empowerment within me. They carried a resonance, reminding me that I was not a passive participant in my life; I could shape my experience through my intentions. The following week, I manifested positive interactions with clients, opportunities for growth, and a renewed sense of joy.

Essentially, the act of cultivating positive intentions helped me create a roadmap, one that each day led me to new opportunities. I began to believe firmly that intention helps shape our reality, and this belief became a cornerstone of the energy I shared during my hairdressing appointments.

In exploring how to cultivate positive intentions, I recommend specific journaling exercises that encourage reflection and visualization. The first exercise is simply called "Clarifying Intentions." Begin by sitting in a quiet space, closing your eyes, and taking several deep breaths. Let go of any distractions, focusing solely on your inner self. Ask yourself: What do I want to attract in my life? Do I seek love, abundance, healing, or growth? Once you have this clarity, write it down in your journal in the present tense as if it's already occurred. For example: "I attract loving relationships into my life" or "I create abundance and joy in my work."

As you write, visualize the energy associated with that intention. Imagine what it would feel like to embrace this reality. Allow yourself to immerse in that feeling, letting it expand within you. Each day, revisit these intentions, read them aloud, and feel the possibility of them manifesting. Over time, you'll notice a shift in your mindset as you open up to the positive energies orbiting your life.

Another powerful exercise is "Gratitude Journaling." Each evening, take time to reflect on the positives of the day no matter how small. Whether it was a compliment you received, a productive conversation, or even just a moment of laughter, write these moments down. Acknowledging the positives helps to shift your mindset and integrates gratitude into your intentions. As you cultivate gratitude, you naturally open yourself up to more positivity.

In periods of struggle, when negativity feels overwhelming, the exercise "Reframing Challenges" becomes particularly helpful. Write down a challenge you're facing and then explore how that challenge can be reframed into a learning opportunity. For example, if you've received critical feedback at work, acknowledge your discomfort before framing it as a stepping stone for growth. This practice not only cultivates positivity but empowers you to take ownership of your narratives.

As I dedicated more time to reflecting on my intentions through these journaling exercises, I noticed a remarkable shift in my interactions with clients. One client, named Amira, revealed during our session that she often felt unworthy of love and success. As we layered her hair with highlights, I shared the importance of cultivating positive intentions and how they had transformed my perspective on life. With a gentle smile, Amira listened, intrigued.

"I never thought about it that way," she admitted, her hands nervously playing with a strand of hair. "I'm always focusing on what I'm lacking, on where I'm failing."

"Let's try something," I suggested, lifting my hands as we moved to the next phase of her hairstyle. "What if, for today, we focus on what you want to attract? You may not feel ready to embrace it all, but allow yourself to express it."

With each stroke of the brush, I encouraged her to visualize her intentions, sharing my own affirmations along the way. "Let's say together: 'I am deserving of love and fulfillment, and I attract positive relationships into my life.'"

By the end of her appointment, Amira emerged not just with a new hairstyle but with renewed intentions painted across her heart. I could sense the warmth radiating from her, the shift in her energy palpable. As she booked her next appointment, I could see the spark igniting within her. We had transformed her session into a space for empowerment and connection through the collective energy of intention.

In opening my heart to help clients frame their own intentions, I learned to cultivate my own positive energy right alongside them. I encountered moments when self-doubt threatened to infiltrate my journey. I occasionally faced stripped days when negativity seeped in during my appointments. It became clear that maintaining a positive mindset requires working in tandem; it's a continuous practice of reinforcing that energy through the people I connected with.

In realizing this interconnected exchange , I often referred to the principles of reciprocity in my relationships. Whenever I felt those familiar waves of doubt, I wrote down a list of my strengths and the positive feedback I'd received from clients. It served as a reminder of my contributions to their healing journeys.

Moreover, I learned that vulnerability is a powerful ally when it comes to cultivating positive intentions. Sharing my struggles openly with clients brought about deep connections and fostered a community of authenticity, allowing others to feel safe in their vulnerability, too. It wasn't just about me sharing my intentions; it was about inviting them to share theirs.

Today, I'd like to encourage you to embrace that vulnerability as you explore your own intentions. You might consider finding an accountability partner someone who can support you as you reflect on your intentions and celebrate your growth. Engage in conversations about your challenges and triumphs. Ask them to share their own intentions, supporting one another in a dance of empowerment and encouragement.

As I conclude this sub chapter , I hope to leave you with a feeling of empowerment. Remember that your intentions have the potential to shape your reality holistically. It's not merely about setting goals but aligning with the energy of those desires each day. As you cultivate positive intentions, you invite opportunities and experiences to blossom in ways that can surprise and inspire you.

Cultivating positive intentions is a journey of self-discovery, a dance of energy exchange between you and the universe. So, take a moment each day to reflect on your intentions, visualize what you want to attract, and open yourself to the flow of positive energy. Remember, you have the ability to create the life you desire, one intention at a time.

The Power of Community Healing

Building a Healing Community

As I sit in my salon, surrounded by the comforting aroma of essential oils and the soft hum of soothing Quran verses , I envision a world where healing and transformation are woven into the fabric of our daily lives. This vision transcends my work as a hairdresser and Reiki healer; it pulses through the very essence of community. I reflect on the power that comes from gathering, on how sharing our stories, our struggles, and our victories can catalyze profound change not just within ourselves, but also within the collective.

Building a healing community starts with recognizing the inherent strength in our connections. Each one of us has a unique journey, and by coming together, we create a tapestry of experiences woven with empathy, understanding, and support. I imagine workshops where individuals can explore their healing paths, share their experiences, and learn new techniques for self-care and energy alignment. These events would not be merely gatherings; they would be sacred spaces where participants feel safe to express their vulnerabilities and celebrate their victories.

One particular workshop I envision revolves around the theme of "Reclaiming Self." Participants would engage in deep conversations about identity, self-worth, and personal history, all while learning practical hairdressing skills that empower them to express their individuality through style. In my mind's eye, I can see the space transformed a room filled with laughter, tears, and heartfelt dialogue.

As the sun streams through the windows, casting soft patterns on the floor, participants gather in small circles, sharing their stories. A woman with braided hair that cascades down her back speaks about her struggles with self-image, how her hair has always been a reflection of her inner conflicts. Another, a man with a head full of curls, shares his journey of coming to terms with his heritage and how embracing his natural texture has fostered a new sense of pride. I can feel the energy in the room shift, the collective support creating an invisible bond, lifting each participant higher.

Beyond workshops, I envision creating support groups tailored to different issues such as grief, trauma, self-discovery which would bring people together in an intimate setting. Each meeting would begin with a grounding exercise, a reminder of our shared intention to heal. We would light candles, share affirmations, and surrender our burdens into the energy of the room. The atmosphere would radiate with compassion and invitation a nurturing cocoon where members can speak freely and honestly, without the fear of judgment.

In these support groups, I see myself facilitating discussions, planting seeds of hope in the hearts of those who are struggling. I think about the importance of active listening; how, in these moments, silence becomes a powerful tool, allowing individuals to feel heard. And as we share, our stories intertwine, forming a collective narrative of healing and resilience. Each person leaves with a renewed sense of belonging, an awareness that they are not alone in their struggles.

One poignant moment comes to mind: a young woman named Amina, who had attended several of my workshops, approached me afterwards, tears brimming in her eyes. She expressed how transformational the experience had been for her how sharing her story made her feel lighter and more connected to both herself and to those in attendance. "I've never felt this way supported before," she said, her voice quivering with emotion. "It's as if, in this space, we're all healing together."

These encounters solidify my belief in the healing power of community. They inspire me to develop collaborative events that foster healing and connection while shining a light on our individual gifts. I picture open-mic nights where participants can express themselves through poetry, music, or even dance. As the spotlight hovers over the stage, I can almost feel the electric energy pulsating from the audience a mixture of encouragement and curiosity, echoing the desire for connection.

I envision walls lined with art that tells the stories of community members. Each piece would represent a personal journey, a healing process transformed into visual language. Local artists would showcase their work, creating an atmosphere where creativity flourishes. In this space, art becomes a bridge that connects us, reminding us that our stories are meant to be shared and celebrated.

The power of community healing lies in the ability to amplify our intentions. When we gather with a common purpose, our energy merges, creating a larger force for healing. I think back to my Reiki practice, the concept of collective energy flows seamlessly into the gatherings I imagine. As individuals come together, the energy becomes a powerful force, transforming not just those in attendance, but rippling outward into the larger community.

Emphasizing the collective aspect of healing, I plan to initiate seasonal community events to celebrate growth and transformation together. Picture a summer solstice festival where we set intentions for the upcoming season a day filled with music, shared meals, and group meditations. As the sun dips below the horizon, we would light a fire, sharing stories of transformation, inviting participants to throw written intentions into the flames, sending their hopes out into the universe.

While envisioning these gatherings, I can't help but feel the thrill of possibility. Each event represents an opportunity to deepen connection, to foster a sense of belonging among participants. And in moments of shared laughter and vulnerability, healing becomes a collective experience that enriches our spirits.

I realize, however, that building this community isn't solely about organizing events. It's about cultivating relationships, laying the foundation of trust necessary for growth. In the days leading up to our first gathering, I reach out to potential participants individually, understanding that a personal invitation can be empowering. I share my vision, my reasons for wanting to create this community, and encourage those I contact to share it, spreading the momentum.

In each conversation, I am reminded of the barriers many people face when it comes to community; the discomfort, the fears, and the vulnerabilities that hold us back. I think about those who have been hurt in the past who have felt isolated in their struggles. These reflections motivate me to nurture a culture of inclusivity from the very start. I want individuals to know that they are welcome, valued, and essential to this healing journey we are embarking on together.

As the day of the first gathering approaches, I feel a blend of excitement and nervousness. The inner chatter begins, questioning my capabilities to create such a space. Yet I remind myself that perfection is not the goal; rather, authenticity and connection are what I seek. I visualize the room filled with diverse individuals, each carrying their stories and their light, ready to share in this collective experience.

On the day of the event, the atmosphere buzzes with anticipation as participants enter. The room is adorned with soft lighting and calming decor, a sanctuary designed to welcome everyone. I provide aromatherapy diffusers releasing gentle scents lavender and sandalwood which embrace my guests as they step through the threshold.

126

The evening begins with a grounding exercise, inviting participants to close their eyes and take a few deep breaths. As I lead the group through a few simple meditative practices, I can feel the energy in the room shift, a calming presence settling over us. Afterward, we break into small circles, inviting individuals to share their hopes for the community and what they seek personally.

As stories are shared, I am filled with awe at the courage displayed by each participant. Greg, a quiet but thoughtful man, shares his battle with anxiety and the isolation it has brought him. Sally, a mother of three, describes her struggle to reclaim her sense of self amid the chaos of family life. I listen intently, my heart brimming with compassion as the individuals around me lay themselves bare, opening up to both vulnerability and strength.

Through the exchange, I witness how our shared energy is ignited the collective desire for healing radiating outward. The laughter mingles with tears, as moments of joy and sorrow intertwine, reminding us that we are all human and that we are not alone.

As the night unfolds, I encourage each participant to craft a vision board a visual representation of their intentions. We gather art supplies, from magazines to scissors, and as the room hums with creativity, I can feel the energy building into a beautiful tapestry of hopes, dreams, and aspirations. Individuals express their desires not only for personal growth but also for the collective healing of our community.

One woman, Maya, feels inspired to create a collage that embodies her dreams of community unity, using vibrant images to represent hope and healing. Others join in, creating boards that symbolize their commitment to their journeys some include words like "empower," "love," and "growth." I am filled with gratitude at the openness, creating an environment that invites transformation.

As the night comes to an end, I gather everyone for a closing circle, reflecting on the power of our shared energy and intentions. I encourage participants to take their vision boards home, hanging them in a place where they can draw inspiration daily.

Looking around the circle, I feel pride swelling within me. Each participant has not only shared their stories but has also embraced the community's empowered energy. As I listen to their feedback and thoughts on the evening, I realize this is just the beginning of a magnificent journey.

With each passing event, I hope to cultivate deeper bonds, create more opportunities for collaboration, and invite new members into this healing garden we're tending. As I dream of future gatherings, the ideas continue to flow community potlucks, wellness fairs, art shows featuring local talents, book clubs focused on spiritual growth, and sessions where we explore natural remedies and herbal healing.

In each initiative, my goal remains the same: to foster connection, to empower individuals to step into their light, and to build a community where healing is both a personal journey and a shared experience. Kadybeauty Seer becomes not just a concept but a vision that invites all to partake in the alchemy of shared healing.

Ultimately, I remind myself that our collective energy possesses extraordinary capabilities. When we come together with the purpose of healing, we create a wave of transformation that resonates beyond ourselves. As I continue to lay the groundwork for this evolving community, I hold fast to the belief that our connections will elevate all of us, igniting sparks of change that ripple through our lives and beyond.

In the warmth of our togetherness, I find hope. Together, we're crafting a legacy of healing a community where voices rise in unison, stories unfold like flowers in bloom, and transformation is embraced as a way of life.

Stories of Collective Growth

Each month, I looked forward to my community workshops with a mix of excitement and trepidation. These gatherings where hairdressing met reiki, where conversations flowed gently like the oils I used on my clients' hair became pillars of connection and growth for me and my clients. In those moments, I witnessed an extraordinary phenomenon: the birth of friendships forged through shared vulnerabilities.

One of the first stories that comes to mind is of Mia, a quiet yet radiant young woman whose courage blossomed over the course of our sessions. She walked into the salon for her first workshop feeling hesitant, her eyes downcast, betraying the struggles she faced. A recent college graduate, Mia carried a heavy heart burdened by societal expectations and the pressure to succeed. As I delicately transformed her straw-like hair into shiny, flowing locks, I could sense her energy shifting.

One evening in the workshop, amidst laughter and the scent of lavender, Mia shared her story with the group. After revealing her fears of not knowing her career path, she was met with an outpouring of support. Her fellow attendees, women from various backgrounds, shared their own journeys and the challenges they faced during their transition into adulthood. Each story became a thread in a tapestry of understanding, weaving together different experiences into a vibrant patchwork of solidarity. In that sacred space, Mia found her voice, and it encouraged her to embrace the uncertainty of her future instead of succumbing to fear.

By the end of the workshop, Mia not only left with a fresh hairstyle but also a new community that lifted her spirit. Over time, she became a key figure in our growing circle, often facilitating discussions and even coming up with insightful activities that tapped into collective healing practices. That simple act of sharing her truth opened a door to exploration, self-acceptance, and ultimately, an understanding that her worth was not measured by her success.

Then there was Linden, a middle-aged man who approached our workshop with a demeanor that screamed, "I'm here only because my wife dragged me." His idea of hairdressing was simply a haircut, devoid of any emotional connection. But through the encouragement of the group, he gradually unfurled layers of his own story about loss, the weight of responsibility, and the emotional cord that had frayed with his aging parents.

As we worked on hair styling tips, I noticed Linden softening. The atmosphere filled with shared laughter and palpable energy, and for the first time, he allowed himself to be vulnerable, recounting the burdens of his life honestly. The women surrounding him embraced him with warmth. They shared compassion, offering him words of solace and understanding while ensuring he knew he was supported and never alone.

One transformational moment arose when, as if a light bulb had gone off, he realized that the community of women rallying around him could inspire him to be more involved not just in their lives, but also in his own. He enrolled in a local support group for men to discuss emotional wellbeing. Witnessing Linden slowly shift from being a reluctant participant to a proponent of change in his circle reinforced my belief in the healing power present when diverse lives intertwine. Each workshop was an extraction of unspoken fears and triumphs, chi flows uniting fragmented stories into evolving narratives.

A few months later, as I stood amidst the cozy aura of my salon during another workshop, Fatima burst in with a flair that could light the darkest corners. Her infectious energy was palpable, and it was apparent she brought the sun with her. She had just completed a project where she organized a charity event benefiting underprivileged children in our community. It was her way of using the skills she'd honed the styling techniques she learned at my workshops and her tremendous heart to radically impact those around her.

As Fatima shared her story, I witnessed how she ignited the flames of passion in everyone. It wasn't just her own accomplishments she highlighted, but she empowered others to tap into their unique talents and identify how they too could contribute. Her fervor for philanthropy charged the room with ideas, suggestions, and a communal spirit that grew wings.

Inspired by Fatima's example, a few women in the group expressed their interests in volunteering and brainstorming ways to assist her efforts. In the months that followed, the unity among the women expanded into tangible projects. Hairdressing stations were set up in community centers, and workshops for low-income women took root.

This charitable work became a bridge through which my clients began to genuinely know each other outside of our cozy space. The networking that happened during those workshops evolved into a strong foundation in which empathy flourished and support blossomed.

Tragedy struck one of our own during one of the workshops when Loretta, a long-time client and friend of mine, shared that her daughter had been diagnosed with a serious illness. The atmosphere shifted instantly a shared breath of concern spread amongst us, and I witnessed the very essence of collective healing manifest in that room. Each moment in her story resonated deeply, and the other women rallied around her, promising to be there for both Loretta and her family.

We set up a meal train for her family and organized a fundraiser to assist with mounting medical costs. A simple workshop that had begun as an exercise in self-care transformed into a network of collective support. Our contributions, small as they might have been, helped ease Loretta's burden, even if only a little.

There was a palpable sense of strength in the room; everyone stepped forward, eager to lend a hand. Loretta was no longer just a woman coming to the salon for a haircut; she was a nucleus around which love and support circled endlessly. As I watched the women check in on her regularly, share encouraging messages, or just show up with coffee to sit quietly beside her, I felt an overwhelming sense of gratitude for this community we had built.

During the quieter, more reflective workshops, I encouraged the women to lay their burdens bare and connect on a deeper level. In one such session, Ava recounted the untimely passing of her brother, and the waves of grief began to wash over her. But instead of retreating into isolation, she reached out. It was here that the healing collective truly shined; everyone leaned in, validating Ava's feelings and sharing their experiences with loss.

Through their vulnerability, the group provided a rich soil from which mutual healing could thrive. Ava soon found comfort and purpose by blending her grief into art, using her talents to paint portraits of those lost to her. A few women in the workshop took it upon themselves to collaborate with Ava, brainstorming ways to set up an art show to not only honor her brother's memory but also to support other grieving families.

The ripple effect of our gatherings began to grow outward through their actions, unintentional ripples of healing that echoed through our community. Help was offered in various forms, creating a tapestry of connection and collaboration.

My heart swells when I think of the many ways each woman in our workshops touched one another's lives. Each connection was like a thread in a beautifully woven blanket of collective growth, stitching together different perspectives and experiences into a safe and supportive embrace.

I also learned a great deal about the colors of healing as I watched them intertwine trust, compassion, vulnerability, and empathy. Each component was essential to the alchemy that took place as women came together with the intention of upliftment. Every story shared wove a new hue into the fabric of our community; the transformations didn't just occur for one individual but spread outwards.

During one workshop, I facilitated an exercise where each woman would express her dreams, ambitions, and challenges. The variety of stories revealed how dissimilar our paths could be yet how wonderfully intertwined they already were.

Charlotte, a budding entrepreneur with a vision for a sustainable hair product line, joined our circle with a heartfelt urgency to do something meaningful in her life. As others chimed in with encouragement, sharing their networks and resources, Charlotte left with tangible next steps to chase her goals. The collective passion ignited around her blossomed into gatherings where brainstorming sessions turned into calls for action empowering women to elevate each other's dreams as they soared towards the stars.

Witnessing those transformations was an honor and a privilege that doggedly reinforced my belief in the power of collective healing. It further propelled me to create programs that directly enhanced these bonds: women led workshops featuring art therapy, mindfulness, movement, and continued exploration of self-care modalities. By creating intentional spaces where women could gather, listen, and share stories, I saw firsthand the fertile ground we were tending.

As I reflect on the collective growth that transpired from those intimate gatherings, I am overwhelmed by the impact that these women have had on me as well. Their stories, their resilience, their revelations have left indelible marks on my practice and my personal philosophy. The community nurturing we fostered returned to me tenfold, teaching me not just about healing others but also about the interchange of energy as it flowed between us.

Embracing each story and every individual aspect, I came to learn that healing doesn't have to be a solitary journey. It thrives in connection whether that's through hair, through reiki, or through the simple act of coming together to nurture the soul.

I reflect on these stories of collective growth with a grateful heart, knowing that our workshop has become a rich garden in which every flower, every individual, nourishes and sustains the others. Through love, we grew. Through pain, we flourished. And through intentional acts of healing, women creating a supportive community grew into something far beyond ourselves.

As we continue to gather, the ever-evolving tapestry of stories, dreams, and transformations we create becomes a guiding light for all who join. More than a salon, more than a simple series of workshops it's a sanctuary of healing, a family, an evolving journey toward understanding ourselves and each other in the beautiful dance of life.

Challenges and Triumphs

Kady stood at the center of her salon one misty afternoon, the scent of lavender and eucalyptus wafting gently through the air. The soft music she curated played in the background, creating a serene atmosphere for the clients who walked through her doors. Yet, there was a weight pressing on her shoulders, one that made her heart feel heavy as she prepared for the community workshop she had poured her heart and soul into organizing. This was more than just another event; it was the culmination of her vision to create a healing community, a space where individuals could come together to share, heal, and grow. But the path to this moment had been fraught with challenges.

In the months leading up to this event, Kady faced a myriad of obstacles. The most prominent of these was skepticism. She had always believed in the transformative power of hairdressing and Reiki, yet as she began to share her vision with others, she was met with questioning looks and dismissive comments. "Hairdressing and healing? Really? Isn't that a bit much?" some would say, eyebrows raised in skepticism. It stung, especially coming from those she had hoped would support her. But deep in her heart, Kady knew she had to push through.

During one of her quiet evenings, as the sun dipped below the horizon and the golden light filled her salon, Kady reflected on her journey. It wasn't just about hair or healing; it was about community, connection, and the shared human experience. She had watched clients walk into her salon downcast and leave with a renewed sense of self, and she was convinced that these transformations could be amplified in a communal space. Yet, the idea of gathering people who might not share her views on healing felt daunting.

One day, as Kady prepared for a crucial meeting with a local community center to pitch her workshop, her friend and mentor, Amina, dropped by for an impromptu visit. Sensing Kady's anxiety, Amina confronted her. "You're worried, aren't you? About what they 'll think? About their reactions?" Kady nodded, her stomach twisting in knots. "What if it doesn't resonate with them? What if they laugh? I've always been labeled 'the healer' or 'the dreamer,' but what if this is too much?"

Amina smiled softly, her eyes filled with understanding. "Creating something beautiful often invites resistance. Remember, the greatest triumphs often come from facing skepticism head-on. You have this gift; don't let fear dim your light." Those words echoed in Kady's mind as she took a deep breath and reminded herself of her purpose.

As Kady approached the community center that day, she felt a surge of determination. She wanted to foster healing connections among people, to show them that vulnerability could be strength. Yet, sitting across the table from the center's coordinator, she felt a familiar wave of self-doubt creeping in. "It's about energy exchange," she began, "how we can share our stories, our journeys, and heal together." The coordinator turned to her, skepticism etched on her face. "And how exactly does hairdressing fit into all of this?"

Kady took a moment before responding, her heart racing. She imagined her salon full of laughter, shared stories, and the gentle hum of healing energy vibrating amongst her clients and friends. "It's about the connection that forms in that chair, the trust we build, and the energies we exchange," Kady replied, her voice steadying. "When we come together, we can amplify that connection beyond the salon. I want to help people find strength in their stories."

Despite the resistance, the meeting ended with a tentative approval for her workshop. But Kady knew her journey was just beginning. In the following weeks, her mind often drifted back to the faces of the naysayers. The whisper of doubt lingered like a cloud, but something inside her ignited further a resolve to nurture her community even amid resistance.

Kady organized a series of promotional events leading up to the workshop to engage the community. She set up small gatherings in local cafés, inviting people to share their stories over tea and pastries. However, attendance varied some nights the room brimmed with laughter, while others felt empty, the chirping of crickets filling the silence where conversations should have been.

Those quiet evenings weighed on her spirit, and Kady would sit alone in her salon afterward, staring at the empty chairs, wondering if her vision was too ambitious. One particularly cold evening, after a lackluster turnout, she slumped against the wall, battling the tide of despair. But amid the stillness, the spark of resilience ignited.

"I have to focus on the ones who came," she reminded herself, recalling how Marie, a client who attended a prior gathering, had shed tears when she spoke about her journey through grief. The raw emotion and vulnerability that surrounded those moments fueled Kady's fire. Each individual who sat before her in her salon or shared their life with her deserved to be heard, seen, and uplifted.

With renewed energy, Kady rallied her spirits. She invited local musicians to her next event, encouraging them to play soothing tunes while attendees shared their stories. The atmosphere transformed, as people began to open up, and slowly but surely, the community started to bond. Kady realized that the first step to healing was often realizing that you are not alone.

But even then, there were setbacks. Occasionally, she faced pushback from established community voices who viewed her approach as unconventional. "What's wrong with the traditional ways?" one critic questioned, prompting Kady to reflect on the very essence of her work. The world was rapidly changing; healing required a more expansive vision that acknowledged the blending of artistry and energy.

These challenging encounters presented valuable lessons. Kady began to view criticism as an opportunity for growth. She accepted that not everyone would understand her vision, and that was okay. She learned to be patient, staying true to her purpose even if it meant walking a solitary path at times. With every workshop, she found herself not only teaching others but also discovering strength within herself strength that transformed her into a beacon for those around her.

As her community started to evolve, the initial skepticism she faced transformed into curiosity and openness. Each session was a tapestry woven with stories, laughter, and healing energy. Kady often found herself feeling overwhelmed with gratitude as she witnessed profound moments of vulnerability. During one workshop, a young woman named Lila opened up about her struggles with self-identity and acceptance. The room held its breath as Kady guided Lila through an exercise in self-love, inviting her to embrace her uniqueness, just as she embraced the individuality of her clients in the salon. The energy shifted palpably, wrapping around Lila's shoulders like a warm hug, and it dawned on Kady that community healing wasn't merely a goal; it was a journey that transformed them all.

As Kady continued to create events that showcased the beauty of connection, she encountered a setback that would test her resilience even further. Just as the momentum of community engagement began to build, a family emergency called her away, requiring her presence out of town for weeks. The fear of losing the momentum and connection she had worked so hard to build gripped her tightly.

In those weeks of absence, she wrestled with feelings of guilt and disappointment not only in herself but also in the gravity of her work. It was different to be an architect of healing in theory, and she feared that without her guidance, the fragile community bonds might fray. But Kady's spirit refused to waver; she had dedicated her heart to this journey, and she would not allow setbacks to define her.

Upon her return, she organized a collaborative healing circle, inviting everyone back with open arms. Kady was greeted with a warmth that took her by surprise. Friends filled the space, expressing how they had continued to meet and share stories even in her absence. Their commitment to the community blossomed, tied together by the threads of connection woven in Kady's absence an unexpected triumph.

"That's the beauty of community," Kady realized as she sat among them. "It breathes and moves, evolving just like us." Witnessing the resilience of her attendees deepened her understanding of collective healing and fortified her belief in the vision she had fought to uphold despite resistance.

This chapter of Kady's journey was one of profound growth, where challenges and triumphs intermingled into a rich tapestry of healing. The experience reiterated that resistance was not an endpoint but a prompt for deeper exploration. Kady understood that creating a healing community would always come with skepticism and trials, but each was an opportunity to learn, nurture resilience, and deepen connections.

As Kady continued on her path, she emerged not just as a facilitator of healing but as a keystone in a community that shared her journey. She learned to navigate challenges with grace, harnessing them to fuel her dreams instead of extinguishing their flame. Each interaction, celebration, and lesson reinforced the truth she had always known: the power of community is transformative, recognizing that healing happens not in solitude but in connection.

Kady left her salon one evening, a sense of renewed purpose enveloping her like a warm shawl. The voices of her community echoed in her mind, tales of triumph interwoven with struggles that spoke to the beauty of collective resilience. She realized that as long as she remained dedicated to her vision believing in the strength that comes from unity she had already achieved so much more than she had ever dreamed possible. With each challenge she faced, she knew she was not merely building a community; she was sowing the seeds of healing connection, one heart at a time.

Prayers and Intentions

Personal Rituals

As I step into my salon each day, the air tinged with the familiar scents of coconut oil and lavender, I am reminded that this space is not just a workplace it's a sanctuary of healing and transformation. The rituals I practice here are my way of honoring the energy, trust, and vulnerability that defines my connection with each client who sits in my chair. They are more than just a series of actions; they are an embodiment of my intentions, a manifestation of my purpose.

As I prepare for the day, my first ritual begins outside the salon door. I take a moment to breathe deeply, inhaling the fragrant air filled with hopes and stories yet untold. With eyes closed, I visualize the flowing energy that surrounds me and extend my hand toward the entrance, allowing my fingers to sweep through the invisible field. In this gentle gesture, I set a protective boundary around my space, inviting warmth and healing while warding off any negativity that may linger.

Once inside, I create an atmosphere of tranquility. The lighting in my salon is warm and inviting, and I often dim the overhead lights, opting instead for soft lamps that cast a gentle glow. The calming instrumental music fills the background, wrapping around the space like a soothing embrace. In this serene cocoon, I want my clients to feel safe a place where their burdens can be shared, and healing begins.

Next comes the lighting of a white candle. A simple act, but one rich in symbolism, the candle serves as a beacon of light in space. As I strike the match, I whisper a prayer, asking for clarity, guidance, and healing energy to flow through me and into the hearts of those who will grace my chair today. The flickering flame serves as a reminder of the divine presence, illuminating our collective journey. I place the candle on my workstation, its glow symbolizing the light we all seek in moments of uncertainty.

After the candle is lit, I gather my collection of crystals, an assorted array of shapes and colors that resonate with different energies. Each stone holds its own unique vibration and purpose. I select a few clear quartz for clarity, rose quartz for love, and amethyst for spiritual growth. Holding each stone in my palms, I close my eyes once again, feeling the weight and energy pulsing within them. I visualize their healing vibrations flowing through my body, a reminder of the interconnected messages of all things.

With the crystals positioned strategically around my salon, I proceed to my favorite corner, where I have set up a small altar. This is where personal rituals come to life, rich tapestries of culture, intention, and spirituality. On the altar are photos of clients I've served and loved ones who inspire me. There are also offerings of dried herbs, essential oils, and small tokens that represent gratitude for the opportunity to be part of so many incredible journeys.

Each morning, I take a moment by this altar to express my gratitude. I close my eyes and channel my intention into these offerings. I give thanks for my hands that craft beauty, for my heart that holds space for others, and for every connection I have the privilege of experiencing. I invite the energies I wish to cultivate to foster love, compassion, and healing in my practice and in the lives of those who walk through my doors.

Throughout the day, these rituals serve as a foundation upon which my hairdressing and Reiki practice rests. But rituals are not just reserved for the beginning or the end of my day; they are interwoven through every appointment. When a client arrives, I greet them with a smile and a warm embrace, feeling their energy mingle with mine. It's essential for me to assess the room's vibration, to be sensitive to what is unsaid, and to hold space for any emotions that may surface during our time together.

Before I begin any styling, I invite my clients to participate in a brief grounding exercise. This is a moment to breathe, to be present, and to connect with themselves. Together, we take a few deep breaths, inhaling fullness, then exhaling stress. In these shared breaths, I feel the energy between us shift, becoming lighter and more receptive. We create a sacred space, and I remind them that my hands will not only transform their hair, but we also work together to transform their spirits.

As I gather my tools, I lay out my combs, scissors, and brushes with the utmost care. Each tool holds meaning, each one representing my intention to create beauty and facilitate healing. I take a moment to run my fingers over their surfaces, welcoming the intention of each movement I will make. Each snip of the scissors is not just an alteration of hair but a release of energy a letting go of what no longer serves my client.

With each stroke of the brush, I imagine the negative thoughts melting away, replaced by a cascade of self-love and empowerment. I often share this visualization with my clients, encouraging them to see their hairstyles reflecting their inner strength and beauty, a tangible expression of the change they wish to embrace in their lives.

As I work, I infuse my hands with Reiki energy, allowing it to flow as I style. My palms warm, attuned to the frequency of healing. I often silently articulate affirmations while creating: "You are beautiful", "You are worthy", and "You are deserving of love." I find that energy flows more freely when I intertwine my prayers with my actions.

This connection deepens as I begin to engage in conversations with my clients. Our discussions often reveal hidden layers of emotions, joys, challenges, dreams, fears and this reciprocity allows me to adapt my energy accordingly. By being present and attuned to their words and feelings, I facilitate an energy exchange that nourishes both our spirits.

Sometimes, I invite clients to share their intentions for their hair transformation. I encourage them to articulate what they wish to welcome into their lives and what they wish to release. If a client expresses a desire to change for a job promotion, a fresh perspective in life, or simply a reclamation of their power I focus my energy on manifesting those intentions through the hair service. The act of styling becomes a ceremony, each strand lovingly shaped into the embodiment of their desires.

As our time together unfolds, I have learned to listen not just with my ears, but with my energy. There are moments when a silence falls over the room, a peaceful pause that signals the healing is occurring. It is during these times that I remain even more still, allowing the energy to do its work, trusting in the process. My hands navigate the hair, but my heart remains wide open, taking in the stories whispered in quietude, the unspoken words that find resonance in the healing space we've carved out together.

After each appointment, as clients check their reflections, I encourage them to take a moment of gratitude. I prompt them to thank themselves for embarking on their journey of self-care and to acknowledge the beauty that radiates within and without. And as they prepare to leave, I take a final moment to offer a blessing, grounding them in their experience. "May you carry this beauty into the world, may you remember your strength, and may you shine brightly."

I find that these rituals have not only enhanced the healing process for my clients but have also profoundly influenced my own journey. As I weave together strands of hair and intentions, I am reminded of my purpose, feeling anchored and empowered by the sacred work I am privileged to do.

Each day in my salon represents a series of unending cycles, like the ebb and flow of energy that brings life to the universe. Through my rituals, I cultivate a vibrant atmosphere that pulsates with love and healing. My internal reflections encourage me to recognize the depth of this work and the importance of prioritizing self-care and intention in all I do.

I invite readers to explore their own spiritual rituals, to connect deeply with their purpose, and to understand how grounding practices can transform everyday interactions. Whether it's through breath work, intention-setting, or honoring the spaces we inhabit, each person has the power to create sacred moments in their lives. We all have rituals that resonate with us be it engaging with nature, meditating, or carrying meaningful symbols of our intentions.

Reflecting on our journeys, we may find joy in the simplicity of these practices. It may be as simple as taking a few deep breaths before stepping into a meeting, lighting a candle while journaling, or reciting a prayer before an important event. What matters is the intention behind these actions the desire to cultivate peace, love, and clarity.

In exploring our individual connections to rituals, we honor our paths and the stories unique to each of us. Within that exploration lies the potential for growth, healing, and the deepest forms of expression. Embracing our rituals can empower us to navigate the complexities of life, allowing us to remain grounded, centered, and true to our authentic selves.

As I continue my journey as a hairdresser and healer, I encourage those who read these pages to reflect on their own rituals, to ask themselves what brings them joy and connection. In turn, we create a tapestry of shared experiences stories of transformation and healing woven through the threads of our unique journeys.

Let these rituals guide us, inviting us into a deeper connection with ourselves and with one another, illuminating our life's work and the beauty that arises when we share our gifts with the world.

Sharing Intentions with Clients

Kady stood in front of the mirror, taking a moment to center herself before the first client of the day arrived. The early morning light streamed through the salon windows, illuminating the small altar she had created in the corner a collection of candles, crystals, and sage, harmonizing perfectly with her vision of healing. Each item was intentional, charged with the energy of love and hope. It was here that she offered prayers silently, invoking peace and grounding for herself and the souls who would cross her threshold that day.

As her first client entered, Kady greeted her with a warm smile, inviting her to settle into the chair that had seen so many stories, emotions, and transformations. Today, however, was special. This was Sarah's first time in the chair. Kady had briefly spoken to her on the phone, sensing the hesitation that hovered in Sarah's voice like an uninvited guest. But Kady also felt a spark of potential, the kind that nudged her to dig deeper into the connections she forged with her clients.

"Welcome, Sarah! I'm so glad you're here," Kady said, her voice imbued with sincerity as she took a closer look at her client. Everything about Sarah radiated uncertainty: her hunched shoulders, downcast eyes, and the way she fidgeted with the ends of her hair. Kady knew the power of energy transfer, and she could sense Sarah's apprehension like a dark cloud hovering near.

"Thank you. I've been feeling pretty lost about my hair lately," Sarah admitted, her voice a mere whisper as she settled into the chair, clutching the armrests as though they were lifelines.

Kady nodded, her heart swelling with empathy as she began her ritual of connection. "Would you like to take a moment to set an intention for our time together? It can be something simple anything you want to focus on."

At first, Sarah stared, her brows furrowed with confusion. "An intention?"

"Yes," Kady explained gently, pulling a few strands of hair back to assess its texture. "It's a way to anchor our session on purpose. It helps establish a positive flow between us. Whatever you wish to manifest during our time together whether it be clarity, strength, or freedom."

Sarah took a deep breath, her hesitation shifting slightly as she considered the words. "I'd like more confidence, I suppose. I want to feel good about myself again."

"Beautiful intention," Kady said, her heart lifting at Sarah's vulnerability. "Now, let's take a moment together to seal that intention with a little prayer."

As Kady closed her eyes, Sarah followed suit, albeit hesitantly. Kady focused her energy on the love she felt for her clients, the joy she derived from her work, and the spiritual connection that flowed through her hands. "May this time together bring forth the confidence Sarah seeks," she silently declared, envisioning golden light swirling around them, entwining their energies and making space for healing.

Kady opened her eyes, a soft smile on her face. "Whenever you're ready, you can bring your attention back to the room."

As Sarah re-engaged with presence, Kady witnessed a gentle shift in her demeanor. The crease between her brows softened, and her breathing steadied. "Wow, that felt... calming," Sarah admitted, glancing sideways at Kady. "I didn't really expect to feel anything."

"That's the beauty of intention," Kady replied, her eyes shining. "It opens the door to greater connection and understanding. Now, let's see what we can create together."

Transformative moments like this unfurled consistently in Kady's salon, where the alchemy of hair and healing breathed life into her practice. Each client brought their own stories, struggles, and victories, and Kady perceived it as a sacred honor to hold space for them. With every cut, every color, and every style, she felt the interplay of energy between them blossom, nurtured by shared intentions.

Her next client, Imani, had been coming to Kady for over a year. Although she loved her visits, she carried a heavy emotional weight today. With a hesitance that lingered in the air, Imani took her seat in the salon chair, allowing Kady to drape a cape around her. Kady sensed the heaviness in her heart a tumultuous mix of excitement and fear stemming from an upcoming job interview.

"Before we begin today, would you like to set an intention?" Kady offered, her voice threaded with compassion as she tied Imani's hair into a loose bun to prepare for the transformation ahead.

"Can we just focus on me being bold?" Imani replied, her voice laced with determination. "I know I'm capable, but I want to walk into that room as if I own it."

Kady beamed with enthusiasm, gently holding Imani's gaze. "Absolutely. Boldness it is!" Together, they closed their eyes, creating a shared moment that felt sacred against the backdrop of the salon's comforting ambiance.

With each breath, Kady allowed her heart to radiate warmth, envisioning Imani adorned in a cloak of strength. "May every word you speak at that interview resonate with clarity and confidence," she murmured, resonating deeply within her spirit. This collective energy was unlike anything else; it created a foundation for healing and growth that transcended the mere act of hairdressing.

As they transitioned into hairstyling, the atmosphere grew electric. Imani narrated her dreams, fears, and aspirations, revealing what laid beneath the surface. Kady listened intently as she worked meticulously, crafting a chic bob that accentuated Imani's features. The cutting of hair became symbolic, an act of shedding old habits and self-doubt.

"Can I tell you something?" Imani began, her voice steady and clear.

"Of course." Kady looked deeply into her eyes, ensuring she felt seen and valued.

"I've been working on accepting myself for who I am. This job would mean a lot, but it feels like so much pressure. When I look at my reflection after I leave here, though, I feel more equipped to face whatever comes my way. You create magic in this space." Imani's eyes sparkled with a renewed sense of hope.

Kady reflected on this exchange and the power of intentions shared. "It's not just my magic; it's ours to create together. Your boldness is already who you are, waiting to emerge like a beautiful butterfly. My hands are simply here to help reveal that."

Through mutual vulnerability, a deeper connection blossomed. Kady and Imani shared their hearts, their dreams, and their fears, fusing their energy into a moment that transcended the usual salon experience. As Kady unleashed her scissors, cutting away more than hair she cut away doubts, insecurities, and the weight Imani carried.

When Imani gazed into the mirror at her new look, she seemed reborn. The reflection was not just an exterior change; it symbolized her journey of embracing authenticity and confidence.

150

"Wow, I love it!" she exclaimed, a mixture of disbelief and exhilaration enveloping her. "Thank you for this gift."

"It was a journey we took together," Kady replied, her own heart swelling with joy. The energy shared between them was palpable, a tangible celebration of vulnerability, healing, and self-acceptance.

In another appointment, Kady welcomed Helen, a long-term client whose energy often sparkled with enthusiasm, but today felt diffused and distracted. After setting up Helen's hair for a color treatment, she carefully approached the topic of intention.

"Helen, how are you feeling today? What can we focus on? Remember, you can always share your prayers or intentions."

With a heavy sigh, Helen confessed, "I feel overwhelmed. Life has just been pushing me in all directions. Sometimes, it feels like my own joy is slipping away."

Kady took a deep breath, recognizing the emotional weight in Helen's words. "Let's shift that energy together. How about we set your intention to reclaim your joy not just for today, but as a reminder of who you really are?"

"Yes! That sounds perfect," Helen said, her eyes lighting up even as tears brimmed dangerously close.

Kady smiled warmly and took them into a sacred silence. Focused on their shared intention, she envisioned radiant light cascading around them, a glowing reminder that joy is innate, even amidst the storm.

"May we honor and reflect on your joy today. Let's bring that spark back to your beautiful spirit," Kady whispered, feeling the electricity charge in the air.

As she mixed the color, Kady took her time, ensuring each brushstroke resonated with love and positive intention. Together, they conversed about joy, laughter, and the little moments that could light up their busy lives. Helen's laughter gradually returned, threading joy back into her spirit like an uplifting melody.

With each stroke of Kady's brush, Helen's hair became a canvas of renewal, embodying the intention they had set. Reflecting on the times they'd shared in the chair, Kady couldn't help but admire how these intimate moments allowed both stylist and client to evolve through collective healing.

Once Helen's hair was washed, colored, and blown out to perfection, Kady turned her around for the reveal. With ribbons of golden highlights catching light, she gasped in delight. "I feel like a new person! Thank you, Kady. I don't remember the last time I felt this way."

"Because you are! This joy you're feeling is just a hop, skip, and jump away. It lives within you; it's always been there," Kady reminded her, celebrating the victory of vulnerable honesty.

With each session, Kady began to see that shared intentions were seeds planted in fertile ground. As they blossomed through authentic conversation, clients would often return more fully alive, embracing empowerment, joy, and the journey toward self-love.

There are also moments of challenge that bubbled to the surface a struggle that accompanied vulnerability. During a session with Lisa, a first-time client who suffered from extreme self-criticism, the air felt heavy with unsaid words. Kady approached Lisa tentatively, sensitive to her quietness.

"Lisa, is there a specific intention that resonates with you today?" Kady asked, guiding her through the familiar process.

"I'm just not sure. I've been feeling really insecure lately, and I honestly don't know if there's anything I can do to feel different," Lisa admitted, the deflation in her voice palpable.

Kady gently probed further, "If there's something you could wish for yourself today, what would it be?"

Lisa hesitated but finally murmured, "I suppose I'd want to feel beautiful. Like, really beautiful."

In that moment, Kady sensed the power of shared intention vibrate between them. Together, they took deep, grounding breaths. "May you see your beauty radiate from within," Kady whispered, firmly believing that self-acceptance started with planting the seed of intention.

As she cut and shaped Lisa's hair, Kady shared her own story of self-doubt and the moments she grappled with insecurity. By weaving personal experience into the session, she created a broader tapestry of connection, weaving resilience and hope for transformation.

Unexpectedly, Lisa's eyes sparkled with unshed tears. "Thank you for sharing that. I've never felt that vulnerable with someone I just met. It makes me feel... less alone."

And in that simple acknowledgment, Kady realized the profound gift of shared intentions how the act of opening oneself could cultivate a sense of belonging, a sacred space where healing flourished in their authenticity. The connection created was electric, a bond that transcended hairstyling and crossed into the realms of healing.

By the time Lisa looked in the mirror and saw her transformation, the vibrant cut that framed her face, the delicate hues that enhanced her natural tones she couldn't help but tear up. She was now literally reflecting the blossoming energy they had cultivated together.

"Wow," Lisa marveled softly. "I finally feel pretty."

With a nod of approval, Kady saw how Lisa carried that weight a little lighter now. This work was an extension of love and appreciation for the journey they took together.

Kady thought of all the moments, each interaction, every prayer, every intention shared and felt a surge of gratitude wash over her. Her role was to cultivate hope, confidence, and empowerment through hairdressing while actively expanding the scope of healing by inviting clients into a true partnership.

Listening to each client's journey allowed Kady to witness the delicate fabric of emotional intricacies and vulnerabilities that were often unspoken. Her dedication to building relationships, sharing prayers, and setting intentions deepened their bond.

In creating that space, she filtered out any skepticism or opposition, allowing her practice to flourish through love and understanding. Every appointment became a sacred ceremony a ritual that went beyond combs and scissors, inviting genuine transformation.

Towards the end of the day, as the sunlight began to dip low in the sky, Kady reflected on the depth of her interactions. In sharing intentions with her clients, she had forged connections that transcended the physical realm, infusing her work with deeper meaning and purpose. Each shared intention was an invitation to engage mutually, creating a tapestry of healing woven from the threads of vulnerability, connection, and prayers spoken from the heart.

And so, as the last client left, Kady closed her salon doors, feeling the weight of gratitude in her chest. In that aún moment of quiet reflection, she realized that every intention shared allowed the alchemy of healing to continue much like the hair she styled, vibrant and beautiful, bursting forward with life through the transformative power of love.

A Collective Prayer

Kady stood in the center of her salon, the familiar buzz of scissors and hairdryers replaced by an eerie stillness that felt pregnant with potential. Around her, chairs were occupied by a diverse group of women and men, each a vibrant thread in the fabric of her community. They had come together not just for haircuts and treatments but for a purpose that transcended physical transformation a collective prayer for healing.

As Kady looked into their expectant faces, she felt a wave of gratitude wash over her. This gathering was more than just a salon event; it was a sacred ritual, and she had spent months crafting the experience that would help her clients connect not just with their outer beauty but also with their inner selves. "Today," she began, her voice steady and warm, "we are here to amplify our intentions through collective prayer. Each of you brings something unique to this space, a piece of your spirit that contributes to our healing. Together, we can harness that energy and create a wave of transformation."

She remembered the first time she experimented with this concept. Sitting cross-legged on a mat in her tiny apartment, surrounded by crystals and burning sage, Kady had attended an online workshop on spiritual healing. The facilitator spoke of energy as a collective force, arguing that when individuals come together with shared intentions, the potential for healing expands exponentially. Inspired, Kady felt an overwhelming desire to bring this idea to her salon, where hairstyling met energy work. In her heart, she longed to foster a sense of belonging and interconnectedness among her clients, a sentiment that had been growing within her since her early days as a hairdresser.

As participants began to settle into the rhythm of their surroundings, Kady guided them through a series of grounding

155

exercises. She encouraged everyone to focus on their breath, inhaling deeply through the nose and exhaling through the mouth. The sound of her voice was soothing, weaving through the air like a balm. "Let's connect with the earth beneath us. Feel the stability and grounding it offers, holding us as we embark on this journey together," she instructed.

The atmosphere shifted as the collective inhalations and exhalations resonated in rhythm, a shared heartbeat that pulsated with intention. Kady observed as eyes fluttered closed, faces relaxing in what appeared to be a deep surrender to the moment. She closed her eyes too and focused on her own breath, feeling it connect with the energy around her. In this space, she could envision a golden light enveloping the group, an energy that amplified their individual prayers into one powerful collective intention.

Once everyone had found their center, Kady invited them to vocalize their intentions. "When one speaks their intention, it becomes manifest. However, when we voice them together, it resonates outward and creates ripples of energy that touch the lives of those we may never know," she explained.

The first voice to speak was that of a young woman named Maya, a steadfast regular at Kady's salon who had been through a lot in recent months. "I'm here to pray for healing for myself, for my family, and for an end to the pain that feels so heavy. I want light to surround us, to lift us up," she said, her voice quavering yet resolute.

Kady felt a twinge of emotion at Maya's sincerity. She remembered the many times they had spoken in the salon about the burdens Maya carried the weight of expectations, the pressure of societal beauty standards, and the challenge of personal relationships. This moment epitomized the purpose of their gathering, and Kady knew they would wrap that prayer around Maya like a protective cloak. "Thank you, Maya. We hold your intention close to our hearts," Kady said softly, feeling the collective energy shift as others began to share.

One by one, voices rose, weaving a tapestry of hope and healing intentions. A mother prayed for her son battling addiction; an older gentleman offered prayers for his community, wishing to see love and understanding flourish amid discord. Each intention reverberated through the space, building an atmosphere dense with care and compassion. Kady could sense how their energies intertwined, like strands of a braid fusing together into something beautiful and strong.

As the last voice faded, Kady invited everyone to envision their collective prayers being lifted into the universe. "Imagine them as colorful balloons, soaring higher and higher until they become stars illuminating the night sky. Each intention lights the path for others, creating a constellation of hope that empowers everyone," she urged, her voice imbued with deep conviction.

When they fell silent, a newfound stillness enveloped the salon. For Kady, this was a moment of reverence. She knew that the act of collective prayer wasn't merely about the words spoken; it was about the energy generated a synergistic force capable of invoking deep healing. Her internal reflections swirled as thoughts danced around her aspirations for this community. In today's world, where disconnect had become common, she envisioned a place where individuals could nurture their spirits, uplift one another, and witness the transformation that results from coming together with an open heart.

Kady had often thought about the power of collective energy and how it rippled through the universe, affecting individual lives in unseen ways. She believed that collective prayer could serve as a beacon for change, guiding each participant to greater self-awareness, empathy, and resilience. The testimonials of her clients had provided poignant insights into the impact of shared intentions.

After much encouragement, many clients had shared their stories from a previous communal ritual each a testament to the transformative power of collective prayer. One woman recounted how she attended one of Kady's community events filled with doubt and hopelessness. "That night, surrounded by all those voices and intentions, I felt something shift. I felt lighter. I set my own intention, and it felt like I was heard for the first time in ages. The next day, I received a call about a job I had long given up on, and I got it! I can't explain it, but I know it was a result of what we did together," she had told Kady, her eyes brimming with tears of joy.

Another client shared how the act of collective prayer had inspired her to rekindle relationships within her family that had been strained for years. "I was given the strength to reach out and say what needed to be said. I realized I wasn't just praying for myself; I was one component in a greater puzzle of healing and connection," he reflected.

Kady listened intently, her heart swelling with pride and possibility. The testimonials were evidence of the waves of energy they were creating together tiny transformations that could blossom into monumental shifts in perspectives, relationships, and self-love. It was within these collective gatherings that Kady felt a deeper sense of purpose: to build a community grounded in shared healing and empowerment.

As the room settled back into silence, Kady encouraged participants to express gratitude for one another. "Look around you," she said, gesturing at the people who had become a circle of support. "Each of us is a vessel for love, strength, and resilience. Let us recognize one another for being brave enough to share our intentions and for cultivating this space of healing."

The atmosphere is filled with soft affirmations and gentle exchanges of appreciation. Murmurs of gratitude permeated the air, a palpable acknowledge that they were not just individuals, but rather a united force that pushed against the tides of isolation and despair. Kady felt tears prick at her eyes as she recognized the magnitude of the community they were building together.

To encapsulate the energy of the gathering, she proposed they engage in a final shared practice a collective release. Kady led them through a visualization exercise where they envisioned all negative energies, fears, and hesitations being transformed into white light. As they released these energies together, Kady encouraged them to breathe deeply and exhale any burdens that lingered in their hearts.

When the session concluded, Kady invited participants to imbibe their intentions through a closing ritual. She passed around small, unique stones, each embedded with a particular intention strength, compassion, healing, and love. "As you take these stones home, let them remind you of today's gathering. Whenever you feel lost or disconnected, hold them close and remember the light of our collective prayers," she said, her eyes sparkling.

As the event drew to a close, Kady watched as participants exchanged hugs, laughter, and affirmations. They were energized, illuminated by the light of connection they had fostered together. Kady felt her heart swell with joy as she observed how these moments had the potential to heal not only the individuals present but also their families and the broader community.

The journey did not end here; it continued beyond the salon's walls. Kady envisioned organizing more collective prayer events, workshops combining hairdressing and energy work, and community outreach programs where those transformed by their experiences could give back. She saw them spreading seeds of kindness into the world as they carried the essence of their collective energy into their everyday interactions.

As she cleaned the salon, her heart was filled with an overwhelming sense of possibility. She reflected on transformational moments of vulnerability, intention, and healing, contemplating what it meant for her and her community moving forward. Each action, each shared moment of prayer and intention had the power to amplify ripples of change, inching closer to a future sparked by love, empathy, and connected .

Kady's vision of fostering a healing community had taken shape, and she felt ready to embrace it fully. She understood that in a world that often emphasized individualism, it was the collective spirit that birthed authenticity and belonging. Each prayer whispered, every healing touch exchanged, and every challenge faced together contributed to a legacy of compassion that would continue to unfold and transform lives.

In those moments of stillness, as Kady locked up the salon for the day, she vowed to nurture the connections formed in this space, committed to fostering abundance not just in her practice, but in the souls of the community she had come to love deeply. It was here, in this confluence of hair and healing, that magic truly happened, and Kady was just getting started.

Lessons from the Chair

Wisdom Shared

Sitting in her salon chair, Kady often found herself immersed in an intricate tapestry of stories, emotions, and dreams. Each appointment was not merely a transaction of services rendered but a sacred exchange a moment in which hair transformed alongside heart and spirit. As she carefully combed through her clients' hair, the air filled with anecdotes, laughter, and sometimes tears, Kady learned that the salon was a sanctuary for stories waiting to be told. It was here, amidst the whir of hairdryers and the scent of essential oils, that she discovered the profound wisdom her clients carried within them.

One afternoon, as sunlight poured into the salon, illuminating motes of dust that danced in the air, Kady welcomed a new client, Aisha. Aisha had been referred by a mutual friend who spoke highly of Kady's work and warmth. As they settled into conversation, Aisha revealed that she was navigating a significant life transition her daughter had just left for college, and she was grappling with feelings of emptiness and uncertainty.

"I feel lost in this new chapter," Aisha confessed, her voice trembling slightly. "It's like I've spent all these years being a mother, and now I have to figure out who I am beyond that role."

Kady nodded, her hands gentle as they glided through Aisha's hair. "It sounds like a profound shift. What are your passions? What brings you joy?"

Aisha paused, considering Kady's question. "I used to love painting. I haven't picked up a brush in years. I guess I forgot about that part of me."

As Kady began to shape Aisha's hair, she felt the energy in the room shift. The act of transforming Aisha's hair became a canvas for Kady to encourage her to reclaim her lost identity. With each snip of the scissors, they laughed, reminisced, and explored the depths of forgotten dreams. By the end of the appointment, Aisha's hair radiated beauty, but what illuminated her face was the spark of inspiration rekindled.

"Thank you," Aisha said, her eyes glistening with gratitude. "I feel lighter, like I can breathe again."

As she left, Kady reflected on how this moment was more than just a haircut; it was a reminder of the power of rediscovery. Listening to Aisha's story had allowed Kady to help her embrace her identity anew. The lessons shared in the chair went both ways; Kady learned to trust in the process of transformation, recognizing that healing requires not just skill but also kindness and empathy.

Another memorable experience unfolded with a long-time client, Janet, who entered the salon with an energy that seemed more subdued than usual. As Kady wrapped a cape around her, she noticed the flicker of worry in Janet's eyes.

"What's on your mind today?" Kady asked, genuinely curious.

"Oh, just work stress," Janet sighed. "I've been feeling overwhelmed and underappreciated. It feels like I'm running on a hamster wheel."

Kady took a moment to consider her response, reflecting on her own experiences with feeling undervalued. As she began to brush through Janet's hair, she chose her words carefully. "It's so easy to forget our worth in the grind of everyday life. Have you taken any time for yourself lately?"

Janet looked thoughtful. "Not really. I don't want to feel selfish, but I'm just so drained."

Kady smiled gently, knowing that feeling selfish in self-care is a pervasive struggle many clients faced. "Prioritizing your well-being is not selfish it's essential. Maybe start with small moments. A warm bath, a stroll in nature, or even just ten minutes of silence to breathe."

As Jana's hair transformed from a frizzy mass into soft waves, the conversation shifted. With each style, Kady encouraged Janet to visualize shedding the weight of her stress. Janet began opening up, sharing concerns about her evolving role at work and her desire to create boundaries.

Kady encouraged her: "It sounds like you've been carrying a lot. It's okay to stand up for yourself and communicate your needs. Your voice matters."

When Kady finally spun Janet around to face the mirror, the change was more than aesthetic. Janet's demeanor radiated confidence, the weight of her burdens visibly lighter, infused with a newly found sense of empowerment.

"Wow. I look amazing!" she exclaimed. "And you know what? I feel amazing too. Thank you for listening."

Kady smiled back, knowing the power of being seen and heard. Each time she sat with a client, the reciprocal nature of healing became increasingly evident. In those intimate moments, clients not only shared their burdens but filled Kady's heart with invaluable insights. Listening was a gift that unwrapped layers of understanding, revealing the interconnectedness of human experience.

The stories continued as Kady worked with a client named Marcus, whose life had taken an unexpected turn after losing his job. As Kady lathered his hair with a soothing shampoo, she noticed the weight of concern etched upon his face.

"Everything feels uncertain right now," Marcus admitted, the tension in his shoulders apparent as Kady gently massaged his scalp. "I thought I had my future figured out, but now… I just don't know."

Kady paused, the warm water providing a grounding connection. "It's understandable to feel lost, especially after a sudden change. Have you allowed yourself the space to process it all?"

Marcus's voice wavered. "Not really. I've just been applying for jobs, but I don't feel like I'm moving forward."

Nurturing the healing atmosphere, Kady shared her own experiences of uncertainty and transformation. "Sometimes, pauses can be an invitation to explore what truly fuels your passion. What lights you up?"

With each word exchanged, Kady's intuition guided her hands, weaving together hair and heartfelt conversation. As the water cascaded down, Republic Marcus began to express his interests in photography and cooking, pursuits he had shelved for too long.

"I used to love capturing moments," he said, a hint of excitement breaking through his gloom.

"Why not take this time to rediscover those passions while you're searching for a new job?" Kady suggested. "Creating something beautiful can also be healing."

As Kady shaped his hair into a fresh cut, it felt like they were both shedding old expectations. When she spun him around to face the mirror, Marcus's smile was brighter. "I needed this. Thank you for reminding me of who I really am."

The wisdom imparted through these exchanges was a gentle reminder for Kady that healing is woven into the fabric of everyday life. In her capacity as a stylist, she was often a confidante a role that came with great responsibility and privilege. As she reflected on each session, Kady recognized that listening was an art form; it transcended mere words and transformed into pure understanding.

One quiet evening, as the last client left and the salon dimmed its lights, Kady sat reflecting on her day. The stories she had encountered echoed in her heart, leaving traces of lessons learned and an appreciation for the profound wisdom hidden in each client's journey. Kady cherished how her clients had unwittingly become her teachers, revealing the beauty of their vulnerabilities and insights.

With the flick of a comb, she remembered her early days in the salon a time when she approached hairdressing solely as a skill to master. The lessons she absorbed as she honed her craft were essential, but it was this deeper layer of connection that made her work truly transformational. As Kady examined her own evolution, she realized that every exchange brought new insights one could never be the same stylist twice.

On a particularly busy Saturday, Kady was joined by a client named Lena. Lena was an energetic woman whose laughter always filled the salon. But this time, as Kady combed through Lena's thick curls, she noticed a heaviness in her spirit.

"Hey, what's going on?" Kady asked, concerned.

Lena hesitated. "I've just been feeling overwhelmed with family responsibilities. My parents are aging, and I feel like I'm constantly juggling everything while trying to keep a career afloat."

Kady appreciated Lena's openness. "That sounds like a heavy load. How do you take care of yourself amidst it all?"

"I don't," Lena admitted, looking quite vulnerable. "I'm just so busy being everything for everyone else that I forget I'm important too."

Kady let her comb rest for a moment, allowing the weight of Lena's words to sink in. "It's crucial to carve out time for yourself, even if it's just a few minutes a day. Your well-being is the foundation that holds everything else together."

As Kady snipped and styled Lena's hair, she encouraged her to voice her frustrations to be honest about her feelings with her family. They discussed boundaries, the importance of self-care, and the myriad ways Lena could simplify her life. By the end of the appointment, Kady could see a different light in Lena's eyes, a flicker of empowerment.

"Thank you for reminding me to prioritize myself," Lena said, beaming at her reflection. "I needed this kick-start to reclaim my life."

As the cycle of appointments continued, Kady found herself drawing from the insights shared by her clients. It taught her that healing was indeed a reciprocal process where both stylist and client expanded through each interaction. The wisdom shared was a source of energy flowing both ways a vibrant channel of understanding and transformation.

Another poignant moment arose when Kady found herself working with Sarah, a young mother who had just gone through a difficult divorce. Sarah approached the chair with trepidation, her shoulders hunched as if carrying a heavy burden.

"I haven't had my hair done in ages," she confessed, her voice trembling. "Everything feels dark."

Kady offered her a warm smile, inviting her to share. "You're in a space of change. What would you like to let go of today?"

"I want to shed the heaviness of this divorce," Sarah said, tears brimming in her eyes. "I just want to feel lighter and more like myself."

As Kady transformed Sarah's hair into a lighter, revitalizing style, she felt the connection deepen. The scissors danced with intention, each cut a release of pent-up emotions. Kady encouraged Sarah to voice her fears, and as she did, the salon became a sanctuary where vulnerability was embraced and healing took place.

"Thank you for letting me express all of this," Sarah said, her voice filled with emotion. "You have no idea how much it means to be able to talk about it."

In that moment, Kady recognized the power of listening fully, allowing each client to unfurl their stories. The wisdom shared transformed not just hairstyles but heart spaces. What transpired in her chair went beyond beauty; it was about reclaiming identity, self-worth, and empowerment.

As the years passed and Kady's clientele grew, she often engaged in discussions about dreams, fears, and vulnerability. She encountered clients grappling with personal loss, career changes, health scares, and the sheer chaos of life. Each story, infused with emotional depth, served as a lesson in resilience and growth.

Kady often found herself reflecting on the nuances of human experience, aware of the complexities woven within every hair appointment. Each chair became a vessel for healing, a testament to the indomitable spirit within her clients who dared to share their journeys. In return, she felt the joy and privilege of being a healer in her own way.

As she prepared for another day at the salon, Kady marveled at the transformational power of connection through stories. The wisdom shared between stylist and client illuminated the path of mutual growth and healing, a bond forged by vulnerability and understanding.

With each appointment, Kady was grateful for the life lessons imparted to her in the sacred space of her salon. The heart of her practice lay in the realization that every exchange was an invitation to learn, grow, and heal together. Through the artistry of hairdressing intertwined with the energy of Reiki, Kady continued to shape beauty, not just in appearance, but in the spirits of those who graced her chair.

Transformational Conversations

As Kady settled into her salon chair, she took a deep breath, welcoming the familiar scents of lavender and eucalyptus that wafted through the air. The lighting was soft and inviting, the walls adorned with photographs of her clients, each capturing a unique moment of transformation. Today, as she prepared for the appointments ahead, she felt a gentle anticipation in her heart, knowing that each conversation held the potential to ignite profound change not just for her clients, but for her as well.

The first client of the day was Mariama, a young woman with a bright smile that contrasted sharply with the heaviness in her eyes. Kady had been styling Mariama's hair for several months, and during each visit, the conversation would take unexpected turns, revealing layers of vulnerability masked by daily smiles. She remembered the first time Mariama sat in her chair, her story spilling forth as easily as the strands of hair that fell to the ground.

"I never realized how much I needed this," Mariama had confessed during their first session together. "I thought coming here was just about the hair, but it feels like… like therapy."

Kady smiled, remembering how the young woman had shifted in her seat, a mix of nervousness and relief. "It is a form of therapy," Kady had replied, adjusting her tools. "Sometimes we just need a space where we can let our hair down literally and metaphorically."

Their conversations often meandered through Mariama's life, touching on her dreams and disappointments, her fears and hopes.

Today, however, something felt different. As Kady combed through Mariama's curls, she sensed a pivotal moment approaching. The conversation took a turn when Mariama hesitated, biting her lip as she sought the words to share.

"I've been feeling really lost lately, Kady," she finally said, her voice barely above a whisper. "Every time I think I'm getting somewhere, something pulls me back."

Kady paused, her heart clenched with empathy. "What do you mean?" she asked gently, aware that this was no small revelation.

"I was supposed to start this internship next month, something I really wanted," Mariama said, her voice trembling slightly. "But then my mother fell ill. I can't leave her right now. I feel torn."

Kady listened, her hands stilling as she processed Mariama's words. Each client's struggle resonated deeply with her, and in this moment, she felt the weight of Mariama's choices. "That sounds incredibly difficult. You are being so strong," she said, her tone reassuring. "It's okay to put family first."

Mariama nodded, her eyes shining with unshed tears. "I just feel like I'm sacrificing my future for my family. Like I'm stuck, Kady."

Kady leaned forward, her heart swelling with the need to comfort her. "Stuck is often where the real magic begins," she replied, her voice filled with warmth. "Sometimes, when we feel trapped, it can lead us toward a path we never expected."

The conversation unfolded like a beautiful tapestry, weaving their shared feelings of doubt and longing together. Kady recalled her own struggles, candidly sharing her experiences of fear and uncertainty while chasing her dreams. With each word, she witnessed Mariama's expression change, a flicker of hope igniting within her.

"I never thought of it that way," Mariama admitted, a slow smile breaking through her earlier melancholy. "I guess I just have to trust the journey… and that it's okay to pause."

Kady's heart felt full, knowing that in sharing their vulnerabilities, they created a safer space for healing. "And I believe that by being there for your mother right now, you're still nurturing part of yourself. Your journey is simply taking a different path."

As Mariama's curls transformed into a stunning braided crown, the two women shared laughter and insights, each moment echoing the importance of storytelling in the healing process. Mariama left that day with a renewed sense of purpose, her spirit lighter and her heart brimming with possibilities.

On another day, Kady welcomed a new client, a middle-aged woman named Leila who walked into the salon with an air of caution. Her graying hair was pulled back tightly, and her attire mirrored a lifetime of practicality over indulgence. Kady sensed a deeper story hidden behind those weary eyes.

As she began to cut Leila's hair, Kady engaged her in gentle conversation. "How are you feeling today?"

Leila's shoulders relaxed slightly, but her smile remained tentative. "I just wanted a change," she replied, her voice carrying a weight of unspoken words.

"What kind of change?" Kady asked, her curiosity piqued as she continued to shape the silhouette of Leila's hair.

"A transformation," Leila murmured, her gaze drifting. "I used to love coloring my hair, trying out different styles, but somewhere along the way, I lost myself."

Kady nodded, sensing the heaviness embedded in Leila's statement. "It's easy to forget who we are amidst life's demands. What inspired you to come back now?"

"I hit a point in my life where I realized I've been living for others, like it's my duty to stay small… to keep everyone else

171

comfortable," Leila admitted, her voice trembling. "But I'm tired. I want to reclaim my joy, my identity."

Kady felt her heart leap. "That's beautiful, Leila," she encouraged. "What does that joy look like for you?"

Leila smiled wistfully, her eyes sparkling with dreams once buried. "I want to wear bright colors again, feel the sun on my skin, and just... be me. I want to step out of this box I've been living in."

Kady could feel the authenticity radiating from Leila. The conversation unfolded, rich with shared moments and sincere connection, as Kady guided Leila through the process of rediscovering herself. They talked about the importance of self-expression, the colors that symbolized growth, and the freedom that came with embracing their true selves.

By the end of their appointment, Leila's hair had transformed into a vibrant auburn hue that matched the spirited woman beneath the surface. As she looked at her reflection, a smile blossomed on her face, radiating with newfound confidence. "Thank you, Kady. I feel like I'm coming back to life!"

Kady's heart swelled with joy, knowing that their conversation had played a part in that metamorphosis. "You deserve every bit of this joy," she replied, feeling the warmth of their connection, both as stylist and healer.

Through each interaction, Kady consistently witnessed how the power of conversation and vulnerability became the foundation of healing. With her next client, a college student named Amina, Kady found herself on another similarly transformative journey.

Amina, though young, carried a heaviness as she sat in the chair, her long hair spilling like dark silk over her shoulders. "I'm not sure why I'm here," she admitted, gazing into the mirror. "I just feel really overwhelmed."

As she began sectioning Amina's hair for a fresh cut, Kady looked into those vulnerable eyes, providing a safe harbor for her client to let down her guard. "What's been overwhelming for you?"

Amina took a deep breath, allowing a flood of words to tumble out. "School is stressing me out. I'm trying to navigate relationships and figure out what I want to do with my life, but I feel lost. Sometimes, it feels impossible to keep going."

Kady felt an intuitive pull to guide Amina through this moment of distress. "It's okay to feel lost sometimes. It's a part of growth. What do you think is scaring you the most?"

"Not knowing what's next," Amina replied, her shoulders tensing. "I feel like I'm supposed to have everything figured out, but I don't."

Kady nodded, her heart aching with empathy. "It's important to remember that life is like this beautiful journey, filled with unexpected turns. You don't have to have it all figured out right now."

As she created soft layers in Amina's hair, Kady shared her own stories of uncertainty during her college years, explaining how those moments led to some of her most precious discoveries. "It's okay to explore. It's okay to try things out and see what feels right for you."

With each trim, Amina's expression softened. "You really think it's okay to not have everything sorted out?" she asked, her voice lightening.

"Absolutely." Kady smiled, feeling a connection that transcended the traditional stylist-client relationship. "Sometimes, it's in those uncertain moments that we find our true selves."

By the time Amina looked in the mirror, she saw not just a fresh hairstyle but a spark of hope lighting up her eyes. "I think I needed to hear that. Thank you for listening."

"I'm glad I could be here for you," Kady replied, her heart full as she waved goodbye to a young woman who was just beginning to embrace her own journey.

As the days went on, Kady continued to engage in transformative conversations that illuminated her spirit. One particularly memorable session unfolded when she met Zara, a client grappling with self-esteem issues after a challenging breakup.

Zara sat in the chair, running her fingers through her hair, eyes downcast. Kady could see the defeat radiating off her, and she recognized the familiar heaviness. "What brings you here today?" Kady asked softly, sensing the subtext of Zara's visit.

"I thought changing my hair would change how I feel," Zara admitted, her voice barely audible. "But honestly, I feel like I'm just trying to hide."

Kady understood the pain behind those words. "What do you think you're trying to hide from?" she wondered, hoping to peel back another layer.

Zara took a deep breath, and tears glistened in her eyes. "It's hard to explain. I just feel invisible. After my relationship ended, I lost a big part of myself. I don't remember what made me feel beautiful anymore."

Kady felt a deep empathy blossom within her. "You are not invisible. Sometimes, we just need to reconnect with what makes us feel seen. What do you love about yourself?"

The dialogue that followed was heartfelt and raw, as Zara bravely shared her insecurities and fears. Kady listened attentively, imparting words of kindness along the way, affirming Zara's beauty and strength. "You're so much more than your relationship," Kady reminded her gently. "You have the power to rediscover your own light."

174

By the end of the appointment, Kady had crafted a stunning asymmetrical cut that embodied Zara's fierce spirit. As they surveyed the transformation, Zara's reflection revealed a glimmer of confidence returning. "Thank you, Kady. I think I needed this more than just a haircut."

"It's a new beginning," Kady said, feeling grateful for the opportunity to be part of this chapter in Zara's life. "Embrace it."

That night, as Kady reflected upon her day, she felt a sense of gratitude wash over her. These conversations had shaped her perspective, encouraging her to embrace her own vulnerabilities more fully. She realized that the exchange between hairdressing and healing was a dance a sacred art of storytelling and connection that created growth and understanding.

The more Kady leaned into authentic dialogues with her clients, the more of her own journey unfolded. She recognized the transformative power of vulnerability: how it dissolved barriers and built trust, how it anchored her in deep compassion, allowing healing energy to flow freely. Each conversation taught her that through listening, sharing, and creating brave spaces for expression, she could empower others to find their truths.

In those moments of collective vulnerability, Kady became aware that the act of hairdressing transcended mere physical transformations. It was a conduit for emotional work, spiritual growth, and soul connection. Each client was not simply sitting in her chair; they were co-creators of an experience that resonated with the heartbeat of healing.

Thus, Kady embraced her role as both a hairdresser and a healer, an alchemist of hair and stories interwoven with love. In that sacred chair, she learned that every stroke of the scissors could illuminate the complexities of life, and each revelation could spark compassion and resilience, nurturing a community of empowered individuals.

With every transformational conversation, Kady not only healed her clients, but she discovered pieces of herself she had thoughtfully left behind but had been waiting to be unearthed. Through storytelling and connection, the magic of her art continued to unfold, shining a light on the boundless realms of growth, healing, and authentic self-expression.

Creating Your Own Alchemy

Practical Exercises

In the quiet moments before I begin a session in my salon, I often find myself reflecting on the transformative power of intention and self-care. Just as every strand of hair tells a story, so too does every thought, feeling, and creative impulse we hold within us. With this notion, I invite you on a journey of self exploration's an invitation to delve into the rituals and practices that have shaped my life and work. Through these practical exercises, I hope to inspire you to create your own alchemy, a beautiful fusion of healing, artistry, and personal growth.

Guided Visualization Exercise

Visualization is a powerful tool that allows us to tap into our inner landscape, bridging the gap between our aspirations and reality. To begin this exercise, find a quiet space where you can sit comfortably. Settle in, close your eyes, and take a few deep breaths, allowing yourself to ground into the present moment.

Imagine a warm light radiating from your heart center. With each breath, visualize this light expanding, filling your entire body. As you continue to breathe deeply, envision this light extending beyond your physical frame, creating a serene aura around you.

Next, bring to mind a specific goal or desire. This could be related to your personal life, your career, or even a creative project you wish to undertake. Picture this goal as a vibrant image in your mind's eye. What do you see? What emotions does this vision evoke? Let yourself fully immerse in the experience, feeling the excitement and joy of achieving this desire.

As you visualize, consider the steps you need to take to manifest this goal. What actions can you commit to in order to bring this vision to life? Allow these thoughts to bubble up without judgment. Picture each action as a stepping stone, each one leading you closer to your destination.

After spending a few minutes in this visualization, gently bring your awareness back to your physical surroundings. Open your eyes, take a deep breath, and jot down your experience in a journal. Describe the images that came to you and the feelings that arose. This exercise acts as a beacon, guiding you toward your goals with clarity and intention.

Journaling Prompts for Self-Discovery

Writing has been my sanctuary, a space where I can articulate my thoughts, feelings, and dreams. In journaling, I invite you to explore the depths of your own experience with the following prompts. Set aside time in a cozy nook, perhaps with a cup of tea or your favorite music playing softly in the background.

1. What does beauty mean to me?

Reflect on your personal definition of beauty. Consider how it relates to your self-image, your values, and how you express yourself in the world. What does beauty feel like, and in what moments do you feel most beautiful?

2. In what ways do I nourish myself?

Take stock of the practices that support your well-being, both physically and emotionally. Write about the activities that energize you, as well as those that drain your spirit. How can you cultivate more of what nourishes you?

3. What fears do I hold that prevent me from pursuing my passions?

Acknowledge the fears that linger in your mind. Write them down, giving them space to be heard. In doing so, consider how you can shift these fears into motivation what steps can you take to confront them?

4. Describe a moment when I felt empowered.

Recall a specific memory where you felt a surge of empowerment. Describe the situation, the emotions you experienced, and the impact it had on your sense of self. Reflect on how you can recreate that feeling in your life today.

5. What does self-care look like in my daily routine?

Document your current self-care practices. What do you prioritize, and how does it make you feel? Are there areas where you can introduce more self-care into your life? Consider ways to elevate your daily routine into moments of intentional care and love.

After exploring these prompts, revisit your writings periodically. This will allow you to observe the evolution of your thoughts and feelings over time, enabling deeper self-discovery and understanding.

Artistic Expression for Healing and Growth

Art has always been a conduit for healing in my life. It opens pathways to express emotions we often cannot put into words. As such, I encourage you to engage in an artistic exercise that combines creativity with self-reflection.

Gather your materials this could include colored pencils, paints, collage materials, or simply a blank sheet of paper. Find a comfortable space where you can let your creativity flow without inhibition. Set a timer for thirty minutes to dedicate to this exercise.

1. Create a Vision Board:

Think about what you want to manifest in your life. Allow your subconscious to guide you as you select images, words, or colors that resonate with your aspirations. Cut out pictures from magazines or print them from the internet, and arrange them on your board.

Focus on how the different elements relate to your goals, dreams, and values. As you organize your vision board, pay attention to the emotions that rise. What do you feel as you visualize your future?

2. Expressive Drawing or Painting:

Let your tools become extensions of your thoughts and feelings. Begin with a blank canvas and allow your intuition to guide your hand. There are no right or wrong choices here; release any judgments.

If you find yourself losing touch with your intuition, consider selecting a theme such as "abundance," "healing," or "transformation" to anchor your creative flow. Allow colors to swirl on the canvas representing your emotions and desires. When your timer goes off, step back and observe your creation. What does it communicate to you?

3. Deepening Reflection:

Once you have completed your artistic piece, take a moment to dwell on its significance. Write about your experience, the feelings that surfaced during the creative process, and how it relates to your journey. How can these insights support you moving forward?

Through artistic expression, you may uncover hidden emotions and truths, fostering self-compassion and understanding.

Grounding Meditation Technique

Sometimes, to create our own alchemy, we need to ground ourselves, connecting our minds and hearts with our bodies. This exercise will guide you through a simple yet profound grounding meditation.

Find a quiet space where you won't be disturbed. Sit comfortably with your feet flat on the ground and your spine tall. Place your hands on your knees or in your lap, palms facing up to receive energy.

Take a deep breath in through your nose, feeling your belly expand. Hold this breath for a moment, then slowly exhale through your mouth, releasing any tension. Repeat this process for a few minutes.

Next, visualize roots extending from the soles of your feet, anchoring deep into the earth. As your roots grow, feel the support of the ground beneath you. Imagine drawing in energy from the earth through these roots, filling your body with a bright, grounding light.

Continue to breathe deeply, inviting this energy to rise through your legs, torso, and arms, filling you with a sense of stability and calm.

After several minutes of grounding, gently bring your awareness back to the room. Wiggle your toes and fingers, feeling the connection to the present moment. Reflect on your experience in your journal, noting any feelings or insights that emerged during the meditation.

Affirmation Practices for Positive Change

Affirmations can be powerful catalysts for change, allowing us to shape our perceptions and beliefs. Choose the affirmations that resonate with you the most, or create your own. You can write them down, repeat them aloud, or incorporate them into your daily routines. Here are some affirmations to inspire you:

1. "I embrace my unique beauty and express it authentically."

2. "Each day, I nourish my body and soul with love and care."

3. "I am worthy of my dreams, and I take steps toward manifesting them."

4. "My fears only serve as guides, leading me to greater growth."

5. "I cultivate connections that uplift and empower my spirit."

As you begin incorporating affirmations into your life, keep a record of your thoughts and experiences. Notice any shifts in your perception or actions as you embody these new truths.

Integration of Practices

The exercises outlined in this subchapter can be woven into your everyday life, creating a tapestry of self-care, intention, and empowerment. As you progress along your journey, remember to stay gentle with yourself. Transformation is a gradual process, and self-exploration often requires both patience and compassion.

To help integrate these practices, set aside time each week dedicated to your personal alchemy. Whether it's a guided visualization, journaling exercise, or artistic exploration, honor this time as sacred. Create a consistent routine where these practices become part of your self-care arsenal a toolkit for healing and growth.

Trust your intuition as you experiment with these exercises. Some may resonate more than others, and that's perfectly okay. The key is to listen to yourself as you engage in this journey. The more you prioritize self-care and exploration, the more you'll unravel the layers of your authentic self.

Final Reflections

As I share these practices with you, I recognize that we all traverse unique paths filled with challenges, triumphs, and revelations. The transformative potential of self-care and creative exploration is profound. Each of us has the ability to craft our own stories of healing and empowerment.

I encourage you to embrace this opportunity to create moments of stillness in the chaos of life, to listen to your inner voice, and to express your truth through various mediums. Alchemy is not merely about transformation; it is about embracing our humanness and honoring our journeys along the way.

Remember, you are the artist of your life. The canvas is vast and open, awaiting strokes of creativity, depth, and meaning. Whether through hairdressing, Reiki, or self-exploration, you have the ability to weave your alchemy a masterpiece of joy, authenticity, and connection. Carry these practices forward as a reminder that you deserve beauty, healing, and growth in all facets of your existence.

Finding Your Voice

Every journey towards self-expression begins with the exploration of the voice within us, the unique cadence that resonates with our deepest truths. As I reflect on my path as a hairdresser and a healer, I understand that finding one's voice is not merely about choosing a style or technique; it transcends that. It is about discovering who you are, understanding your beliefs, and manifesting them through your art. My hope in sharing this subchapter is to guide you on your quest for authenticity, just as I have navigated mine.

At the heart of finding your voice is the understanding of individuality. In a world where trends reign supreme and conformity can often feel like the easier route, the challenge is to embrace your uniqueness. The first step in this creative process is to unearth what truly resonates with you. What do you stand for? What ignites your passion when you think about creating? For me, it was the healing power of hairdressing, the connection I felt to each client, and the stories they brought with them into my salon.

I learned that every strand of hair carries a story, and as I began to listen deeply, my vision expanded beyond the physical transformation. I realized that I was not merely a hairdresser; I was a storyteller, a healer, and a bridge connecting people to their inner selves. The techniques I employed in hairdressing became an extension of my voice, crafted through my experiences, successes, and yes, even my failures.

When I first started my journey, I grappled with self-doubt and uncertainty. I often found myself imitating other stylists, mimicking what I saw on social media, or trying to apply techniques I was not yet comfortable with. The results were often disheartening. I had the skills, yet my work lacked the spark that comes from genuine self-expression. It was a turning point when I realized that I was trying to fit into a mold rather than carve out my own distinct space. The moments I spent replicating others' styles left me feeling hollow and unfulfilled.

So, I made a conscious decision to explore more about myself not just as a hairstylist, but as a person. I began asking myself questions: What excites me about hairdressing? What do I love about my interactions with clients? What are the values that I want to embody in my work? This inner exploration was critical; it opened a gateway to my authenticity and laid the foundation for finding my stylistic voice.

Embracing authenticity also meant acknowledging my roots, the cultural background that shaped me and influenced my understanding of beauty. The traditions shared by my ancestors provided a rich tapestry of inspiration. My grandmother's rituals, the presence of community in haircare, and the spiritual aspects of grooming were not just background noise; they were deeply engrained in my identity. I began infusing these personal elements into my work, allowing my heritage to guide my artistry.

Cultivating your voice takes practice and patience a lesson I learned through trial and error. As I experimented with different styles, I allowed space for mistakes. Mistakes, I discovered, are powerful teachers. They guided me toward clarifying my unique approach and narrowing down the techniques that felt genuinely aligned with my vision. Sometimes a failed attempt at a new style would ignite a spark to create something entirely different, revealing an unexpected direction that resonated with my spirit.

As I adopted this more exploratory mindset, I began to define my signature styles. Each one represented not just my technical ability but also a piece of my heart and belief system. Through designs that celebrated diversity and empowerment, I began nurturing a following of clients who resonated with my intentions. My hairstyling evolved into a form of personal expression, with each client's transformation reflecting a part of my journey and our shared experience.

To assist others in discovering their authentic voices, I developed a series of guiding principles that I still honor today. First, I encourage you to observe what sparks joy in your creative endeavors. Reflect on times when you felt alive while creating or connecting with others. What were you doing? Who were you with? It is essential to identify and lean into those moments. When you distill the essence of what invigorates you, the path to your unique voice becomes much clearer.

Second, embrace vulnerability. It's easy to show your perfected work to the world, but it requires courage to share your process, your growth, and your hurdles. Vulnerability invites authenticity; it affirms that we are all on this journey together, growing and learning. Encourage yourself to be open about your challenges in hairdressing or other creative practices. Connect with peers, exchange stories, and seek feedback. This engagement cultivates a nurturing environment for your growth, helping you hone your style.

The third principle I discovered is experimentation. Give yourself permission to step outside your comfort zone. Play with textures, colors, and forms in your work. Challenge societal norms of beauty and standards. What emerges when you combine unconventional styles? How do you feel when you take risks with your craft? Through this journey of exploration, your voice inherently will shine brighter as you embrace what feels natural for you.

Along with experimentation comes the importance of patience and persistence. Recognize that the journey to uncover your voice is not always straightforward. There will be ups and downs, moments where you feel aligned, and times when you feel lost. It's all a part of the process. Celebrate your small victories, whether they are mastering a new technique or receiving positive feedback from a client about a particular style you created.

Above all, remember that the journey to finding your voice is ongoing. Each hair you style is an opportunity to express your evolution. Just as the hair grows and changes over time, so does your voice. I find myself continually pushing boundaries, inspired by the ever-changing landscape of hairdressing and the personal experiences of clients that come my way. This fluidity embodies the essence of true artistry and healing.

Along my journey, I've encountered significant moments that solidified my voice. One client comes to mind: she was a young woman who walked into my salon feeling lost and disconnected, a shadow of her potential. As we began to converse, she opened up about her self-image struggles and insecurities. Her stories resonated with me, illuminating a parallel with my own experiences.

As I styled her hair, I listened intently, connecting her words to the movements of my hands. I infused prayers into my work intentions of empowerment and self-love as I meticulously crafted her look. By the end of the appointment, she didn't merely sport a new hairstyle; she radiated confidence and vibrancy. In that moment, I felt my voice solidify not just as a stylist, but as a conduit for healing, nurturing, and empowerment.

It is important to engage with your audience as you discover your voice. I remember organizing workshops to share my knowledge and experiences, inviting others to engage in conversations about self-expression. These gatherings exposed me to diverse perspectives, enriching my understanding of individuality and creativity. Each participant brought their essence, and through dialogue, I witnessed how each voice contributed to the alchemy of our collective experience.

The beauty of expressing your voice is that it collaborates with others, forming a powerful tapestry of interconnected experiences. Every person has a unique story that deserves to be told. The more we share and listen, the richer our understanding of ourselves and each other becomes. It is this connection that can inspire transformation, healing, and artistry in ways unimaginable on our own.

The realization that you are not alone in your journey is liberating. The collective energy of those exploring their voices can create a momentum that propels everyone forward. The voices of our communities intertwine, encouraging growth and creating an environment where empowerment flows freely. This spirit of collaboration has driven me to design programs that emphasize community healing, allowing me to give back while inviting others to step into their authentic selves.

As you embark on your quest to uncover your voice, allow your emotions to guide you. Spirit and artistry are deeply intertwined, and expressing your feelings through your craft can lead to profound insights. When I feel uninspired, I turn to my spirituality, using meditation and the practice of Reiki to realign my energy. This journey inward often unveils what I need to express, helping me reconnect with my purpose and the core of my artistry.

In the end, finding your voice is about embracing the entirety of who you are your heritage, your stories, your struggles, and your triumphs. Trust that your voice is there, waiting to be unearthed, and know that it is perfectly imperfect just as you are. Let your voice evolve, recognizing the shifts and turns as opportunities for growth.

As you navigate your personal path, I encourage you to document your progress. Journaling thoughts and ideas can provide clarity and insight as you reflect on your growth over time. Over the years, I've maintained notebooks filled with sketches, notes, and visions of my evolving artistry as a stylist and healer. Revisiting those pages often reminds me of the beauty of the process, each entry embodying a moment of my journey towards authenticity.

Your unique voice is indispensable in a world craving genuine expression. There will always be trends and standard practices, but it is your authenticity that will draw others to you. Embrace it, nurture it, and let it flourish. As we each discover our voices, we contribute to a more healing and empowering narrative for ourselves and the community around us.

The journey to finding your voice can feel daunting, but I assure you, it is one of the most beautiful discoveries you will make. Allow yourself the grace to explore, the courage to fail, and the commitment to learn. Each step you take toward embracing your individuality creates space for healing not just for you, but for everyone you touch.

As you stand in the mirror of your creative expression, remember that your voice is powerful, transformational , and authentic. In every creation, in every interaction, let your voice be your guide, and trust in its ability to create ripples of change and healing. Your unique alchemy is waiting to be revealed, and I cannot wait for the world to witness the extraordinary beauty you create.

Embracing the Journey

The journey of self-discovery and healing is rarely a linear path. It winds and turns, with peaks of joy and valleys of despair, each moment serving as a vital part of the tapestry of who we are becoming. As I sit in my quiet salon, the hum of a blow dryer in the background, I often find my thoughts drifting back to my own journey. The memories are vivid a tapestry of experiences, mistakes, joys, and revelations that have shaped my perspective on beauty, healing, and connection.

When I first entered the world of hairdressing, I believed I understood the importance of aesthetics. I had grown up surrounded by beauty rituals that celebrated our rich heritage moments spent watching my grandmother transform hair into exquisite representations of elegance and strength. Yet, despite my enthusiasm and passion for hairstyling, I was blinded by a single-minded focus on technique at the expense of the deeper connection that I would eventually come to understand. Each stroke of the brush on hair was a creative act, yet it was also a chance to heal and connect on a more profound level.

I can recall specific days in my early career when the weight of expectations, both internal and external, threatened to eclipse my vision. I had longed to be recognized as an artist, a healer, and a transformative force. But there were moments when the beauty of the craft felt overshadowed by self-doubt and insecurity. After all, how could I nurture the beauty in others when I was struggling to embrace my own? The dissonance was palpable, and I often found myself at a crossroads, questioning whether I was on the right path.

As I navigated these challenges, my growing understanding of Reiki began to shape my perspective. I remember my first Reiki session vividly. I had walked in skeptical, hovering between curiosity and doubt. Yet as I lay on the massage table, I felt an unexpected warmth envelop me, leaving me vulnerable yet open to something new. Through that experience, I learned a fundamental lesson: healing is not merely about fixing what is broken but embracing what is whole. I carried this wisdom into my practice, recognizing that my clients' stories were not about their flaws but about their journeys each curl, twist, and braid telling a chapter of their lives.

It was a slow process, one that required constant introspection. Transitioning from being focused solely on aesthetics to embracing the spiritual and emotional dimensions of hairstyling was initially daunting. There were days filled with trepidation as I learned to let go of rigid notions of success, allowing space for vulnerability and connection. With every transformational haircut, I began to see parts of myself reflected in my clients moments of insecurity, snippets of joy, and bursts of laughter.

As I embraced the journey, I started to view challenges as opportunities for growth. There were clients whose hair seemed unmanageable, their histories intertwining like tangled strands. In those moments, I realized that healing began with listening. Listening not only to their words but also to their energy the subtle shifts that communicated unspoken fears and dreams.

One transformative experience involved a woman named Amina, who came to me feeling heavy, burdened by both her literal and metaphorical weight. As she sat in my chair, her shoulders slumped, and her eyes reflected exhaustion. Her hair was a mix of neglect and beautiful potential, much like her spirit. As I combed through her locks, gently detangling the knots, we began to talk. We spoke about her aspirations, her family, and the shadows of self-doubt that loomed over her. With every stroke of my brush, I felt her walls begin to crumble. It was during that session that I fully embraced the notion that my role was not just that of a stylist but also a healer.

Through our conversation, Amina shared how she had constantly sought to please others at the expense of her own happiness. The moment she uttered those words, I was reminded of my own battles with the expectation to conform. I gently encouraged her to shed the weight of those expectations, inviting her to reclaim her narrative through her appearance.

As I sculpted her hair, Amina's energy shifted. The transformation was not merely physical; it resonated through her very being, as she learned to embrace her identity beyond societal pressures. When she looked in the mirror, the beaming light in her eyes told me everything I needed to know. Together, we had embarked on a journey, and the beauty we created was a testament to resilience and strength.

That experience solidified my belief in the healing power of human connection and self-acceptance. It was a turning point for me, forcing me to confront my own areas of growth. I began to reflect on my inner dialogues. Was I extending the same compassion to myself that I offered my clients? It was a hard question, but one that became the bedrock of my inner journey. Embracing the journey meant confronting my perceived inadequacies and shifting my mindset from one of self-criticism to one of self-compassion.

Transformation is a delicate process that unfolds over time, often requiring patience that can feel elusive. I learned to allow myself to experience both the highs and the lows without judgment. Just as I would guide a client through every step of a haircut, I began to guide myself through my own fears and aspirations. I recognized the importance of nurturing my spirit and allowing space for courage to flourish, embracing moments of imperfection as part of the grand design of growth.

Throughout this self-exploration, I developed rituals that grounded me. Daily practices became pillars of my journey, encompassing meditation, visualization, and mindful breathing. These practices taught me the beauty of presence, crucial for both healing and creativity. In those moments, I learned to align my energy, returning to the essence of who I was and who I aspired to be.

There were also times when the shadows of doubt crept back in. Instances arose when clients expressed dissatisfaction, echoing my own struggles with vulnerability. But these moments became foundational in my journey of growth. Instead of retreating into fear, I approached them as learning opportunities. I listened, asking myself how I could adapt, how I could embrace the imperfections both in hair and life with grace.

I'd often remind myself that just as each hair type is unique, so too are the journeys we each undertake. In sharing stories, the conversations often led to unexpected revelations both for myself and my clients. I began to see that challenges lay in the fabric of our experiences, and that authenticity made this fabric richer. Embracing my own imperfections bred deeper understanding, allowing me to lead with empathy rather than judgment.

One profound realization came during my time with a young college student named Leila. She arrived at my salon noticeably nervous, revealing her anxiety about her upcoming graduation and the looming responsibilities that accompanied it. As I began to style her hair, we delved into a conversation about societal expectations, sparking a dialogue about fears tied to identity and the pressure to conform.

Leila's hair had been a representation of her freedom, a cascade of vibrant color that reflected her creativity. Yet, due to the pressure of 'maturity' in the professional realm, she was leaning towards more conservative styles. As I cut away the lengths of her vibrant hair, I found myself breaking the tension with humor, encouraging her to consider how to prioritize her authenticity over others' perceptions. With each lighthearted jab, her face lit up, and it became clear that she had buried her true self under layers of expectation.

By the end of our session, Leila left not just with a haircut, but with a renewed sense of identity and freedom. Much like my journey, her transformation would take time, but that day marked a pivotal moment of reckoning. In my own reflections, I remarked that our interactions had become threads weaving through a collective tapestry, illustrating how our journeys intertwine seamlessly through shared experiences.

As I reflect on these pivotal interactions, I am humbled by the reminder that healing is a mutual process. Each client's journey, filled with battles and triumphs, echoes my own. It is through these connections that I have found my voice as both an artist and a healer, intertwined in the narrative of transformation.

Throughout this book, I encourage you to reflect upon your own journey. Embracing the journey requires patience and compassion, both for yourself and those who may walk alongside you. Allow yourself the grace to celebrate your progress, no matter how small. Understand that healing is not always a beautiful or linear experience; it is multifaceted, often filled with lessons and growth that come from unexpected places.

As you navigate the world, remember that transformation is built on dedication a promise to yourself to nurture your spirit and your passions. Embrace the practice of self-care, creating rituals that infuse your daily life with intention. Know that movement comes from a place of love, and with each step forward, you will hone your unique alchemy, crafting the essence of who you are destined to be.

So take a moment to breathe, reflect on your own journey, and allow yourself the freedom to grow. Transformation beautiful, poignant, and imperfect is waiting for you. Embrace it with open arms, for this journey is not just about the destination; it's about exploring the richness of your path, discovering strength in vulnerability and joy in every twist and turn. Your journey is uniquely yours, and therein lies its beauty. Embrace it.

Building Empathy

As I lean into the rhythm of the hairdryer, the gentle hum vibrating through my hands and the soft scent of lavender-infused oil wafting through the salon, I take a moment to reflect on how my experiences with clients have shaped my understanding of empathy. Each visit isn't just an appointment on my schedule; it's a sacred exchange, a moment where hearts unfold as effortlessly as the strands of hair I sculpt. The salon chair has become a confessional booth, a place where vulnerability is shared, and healing begins.

The first time I truly recognized the power of empathy in this setting was with a client who entered my salon carrying an invisible weight. Her name was Maria, a mother of two young boys, who walked in with downcast eyes and a frown etched upon her face. The heaviness in her shoulders spoke volumes, a testament to the burdens she had been carrying, yet appeared to be invisible to the world outside. As she settled into the chair, the first thing I noticed was her hair long, tangled strands that seemed to echo her inner turmoil.

I approached her gently, asking about the change she wanted for her hair. Her initial hesitation gave way to a cascade of words, tumbling forth like the river that had been dammed for far too long. Maria shared her struggles, her worries about her children, and the relentless pressure of balancing work with home life. Listening to her, I felt an overwhelming wave of compassion wash over me, igniting a deeper connection between us that transcended the role of hairdresser and client.

In that moment, I realized that my hands could do more than shape hair; they could help carry her burden, if only for a short while. As I transformed her hair into a radiant style that framed her face beautifully, I focused on infusing each section with positive energy, channeling my desire for her joy into the very strands I was working with. It was here that I embraced the vulnerability inherent in our interaction; she was opening her heart to me, sharing her fears and anxieties while I lent her my hands to alleviate the burden, even if momentarily.

By the time she rose from my chair, the glow on her face was not simply a reflection of the physical transformation. It was a glimmer of renewed hope, the empowerment that came from being truly seen and heard. That experience lingered in my heart long after she left, reminding me of the profound impact we can have on one another through empathy. It forged a commitment within me to nurture that aspect in all my interactions, not just as a hairdresser but as a healer.

Another instance that catalyzed my journey toward greater empathy involved an older gentleman named Mr. Thompson. He had been a regular at my salon for years, known for his warm smile and kind-hearted nature. However, on a seemingly ordinary day, I noticed a subtle change in him the sparkle in his eyes dimmed, and the laughter that usually bubbled readily from his lips seemed stifled.

As I began his haircut, I let the scissors glide smoothly through his thinning hair while I asked him how his week had been. Initially, he responded with typical pleasantries, deflecting any inquiries away from his personal life. Yet, as I continued to snip away, I gently probed deeper, recognizing the importance of creating a safe space for him to open up. I shared anecdotes of my own struggles, turning the conversation into a dialogue rather than an interrogation.

With each exchange, I noticed him start to relax, allowing himself to peel away the layers surrounding him. Eventually, he confided that he had been grappling with the loss of his wife, a companion he had shared decades of his life with. He never realized how much he had internalized his grief; it was only during that haircut that the tears broke free, cascading down his cheeks. In that moment, I handed him tissues and held space for him, allowing him to release his sorrow.

I remember the weight of his hand resting on mine during that consultation; it felt like a sacred trust. I understood that our shared vulnerability was nourishing a healing experience for both of us. While I was intended to heal his visage, his words soothed my spirit, deepening my understanding of loss and love. With this embrace of vulnerability came an extraordinary realization about the duality of my role how I was not just a stylist, but also a compassionate listener and an instrument of healing.

Empathy, I learned, is not simply an expression of sympathy; it's an active engagement in the emotional world of another person. It requires a profound presence, setting aside my own thoughts and feelings to hold space for someone else's truth. This realization has informed my practice immeasurably. Each time I welcome a client into my salon, I am acutely aware of their unique experiences and the invisible stories they bring with them.

The stories of the individuals who sit in my chair often resonate long after they've left. For instance, there was a courageous young woman named Amina who walked in one dreary Tuesday afternoon looking for her first haircut after a difficult breakup. Her past relationship had left her feeling both defeated and diminished, robbing her of the vibrant spirit I sensed lurking beneath her surface.

Throughout our session, I listened to her reflections on heartbreak and self-doubt as I delicately shaped her hair into a bold new style that matched her vivacious personality. I encouraged her to reclaim her confidence, celebrating the new journey she was embarking on. By tenderly transforming her appearance, I felt I was also aiding in a deeper metamorphosis, one that would empower her emotionally as well.

When Amina finally caught a glimpse of herself in the mirror, the tears that trickled down her cheeks were not born of sadness; they were a release, a declaration of her willingness to embrace the future unencumbered by her past. "Thank you for helping me rediscover myself," she said softly, wrapping her arms around me in a warm embrace.

With every story shared, my understanding of empathy deepened. It became increasingly clear that compassion goes hand-in-hand with authenticity. It was essential that I entered each client interaction as my true self, vulnerably sharing my own stories to foster a collective sense of safety and healing.

In voluminous exchanges with clients, I began to see the threads of commonality among us all our heartaches, aspirations, and moments of doubt. The beauty of human experience lies in connection, and through it, we find healing. I recognized that my own journey mirrored theirs; my search for purpose, acceptance, and love was not unique but shared among many.

My mentor, the gentle Reiki master who had walked alongside me for years, often spoke of the importance of holding space. She taught me that this is not just about listening but about resonating with the emotions of another and reflecting them with compassion. It was in these lessons that I discovered that my role as a healer extended beyond physical touch; it was embedded in the profound acknowledgment of the person sitting in front of me.

A pivotal moment in my understanding of shared experience came when I was working on a community outreach project focused on holistic healing. I had offered free haircuts to women transitioning out of shelters, each of whom carried their own stories of resilience and survival. During one particular session, I met Sarah, a woman whose laughter masked an ocean of sorrow. As she sat in my chair, her hair was testimony to her tribulations neglected and unkempt.

While styling her hair, she shared snippets of her story, woven with threads of sorrow and bravery. She had fled an abusive relationship, leaving behind not just her partner but her identity. As I shaped her hair, I could feel the energy shifting the chair became a sacred place of transformation where wounds were honored.

When Sarah looked in the mirror, her bright smile illuminated the space like sunlight slicing through clouds. In that moment, I felt our shared vulnerability amplify; my offering of hairdressing became a vessel of healing a reminder that beauty rises from resilience. As she left, she promised to share her story with others who needed hope, creating a beautiful ripple effect.

Empathy thus weaves itself into the fabric of my practice. It's what allows me to look past the surface and see the tapestry of each individual who graces my chair. I've learned to cultivate patience to create the atmosphere where the unspoken words can freely flow, allowing me to respond in authenticity.

Through every haircut and every color, I am reminded of the art of connection, the delicate dance between healer and client. Each moment is a lesson in understanding, an opportunity for growth that transcends our immediate interaction. I find joy in being the vessel of transformation, blending artistry with compassion.

Now, more than ever, I invite you, the reader, to explore your own experiences with empathy. Reflect on the moments in your life when you felt compelled to слушать, to heal, or to share your own vulnerabilities. Recognize the instances when you held space for another, knowing fully that your presence was a balm to their wounds.

Consider how you might integrate these lessons into your own life. Empathy is a gift we can all cultivate; it begins with understanding ourselves. Embrace your unique story, recognizing that even in your darkest moments, there is strength in vulnerability. Each individual carries their own burdens, and sometimes, just being present for someone else can be an incredible act of healing.

As you navigate your journey, remember the interconnected essential of humanity the shared threads that bind us in the tapestry of life. Embrace vulnerability not as a weakness but as an empowering force that fosters deeper connections. Your heart has the power to inspire change, to carry hope, and to bring healing in ways that may surprise you.

The journey toward empathy is ongoing; like the seasons, it requires nurturing, patience, and understanding. Allow every encounter to shape who you are, just as each story shared within my salon chairs has shaped my narrative. Together, let us continue to grow, heal, and weave a fabric of compassion that envelops every corner of our communities.

The Journey Continues

Vision for the Future

As I stand in my salon, surrounded by the familiar scents of essential oils and the soft hum of calming music, I feel a sense of gratitude for all that has brought me here. The walls, adorned with vibrant artwork representing my journey and the beautiful transformations of my clients, resonate with the stories of healing and connection we've shared. Yet, each new day presents an opportunity to dream bigger, to envision a future that extends beyond the doors of my salon, one that intertwines the worlds of hairdressing and holistic healing in ways that are innovative and life-affirming.

My vision for the future is rooted in my belief that true beauty radiates from a place of inner wellness. Hairdressing has always been more than just aesthetics for me; it is a sacred ritual that nurtures and heals. As I reflect on my journey, I see a landscape where this philosophy can thrive and expand, impacting not only my clients but the broader community. With this vision in mind, I have crafted a roadmap filled with initiatives designed to empower individuals and foster a collective spirit of healing.

One of the cornerstones of my future aspirations is the launch of workshops that blend hair care with holistic practices. I envision a series of experiential sessions where participants engage not only in hair techniques but also in self-care rituals that promote emotional well-being. These workshops would be designed to create a safe space for attendees to explore their relationship with beauty and self-expression. I want to facilitate an environment where participants can share their stories, illuminating the connections between their inner feelings and outer appearances. By integrating guided meditations, breathwork, and Reiki into these workshops, I believe I can help participants uncover the deeper layers of themselves that have long been overshadowed by societal beauty standards.

The idea of collaborating with other wellness practitioners excites me immensely. I envision hosting retreats that bring together hairdressers, Reiki masters, yoga instructors, and nutritionists, creating a multifaceted approach to healing. Imagine a weekend filled with rejuvenation where individuals can indulge in collective practices that soothe the mind, heal the body, and uplift the spirit. This holistic approach would remind participants that beauty is not a singular experience; rather, it is forged in the intricate union of physical, emotional, and spiritual health.

As I consider these workshops and retreats, I reflect on my personal journey and the lessons I've learned along the way. I remember the early days of my practice when I incorporated Reiki into my hairdressing sessions. At first, I wasn't sure people would understand or appreciate the blending of these two aspects of my identity. Doubt crept in, but just as I learned to trust in the healing energy I channeled, I understand now that my clients responded positively to my dual approach. Their enthusiasm ignited my passion further and reinforced my belief that combining hairdressing and healing could resonate powerfully on a broader scale.

In our fast-paced world, the idea that we can pause and reconnect with ourselves is revolutionary. My workshops would draw on this necessity, encouraging participants to carve out time in their busy lives for self-reflection and rejuvenation. Each session would be a gentle reminder that beauty isn't just skin deep; it is a heartfelt experience rooted in self-love. As people share their stories and participate in healing practices, I trust that they will realize the transformational power of coming together in a shared journey toward wellness.

In paralleling this community-focused approach, I also dream of creating a mentorship program for aspiring hairstylists who wish to explore the healing aspects of the craft. I remember my own struggles early in my career the uncertainty, the desire for guidance, and the hunger to intertwine my passions. Mentorship, I believe, can bridge the gap for newcomers seeking to maintain their artistic integrity while exploring their identities as healers. Through hands-on training, guided discussions, and experiential learning, future hairstylists could emerge not only as artisans but as conduits for healing. This program would emphasize the importance of empathy and connection in the salon environment, nurturing a new generation of stylists who understand the significance of the work we do beyond the chair.

To facilitate these transformational connections, I envision partnerships with schools and community organizations. Collaborating with these entities would allow me to extend the reach of my workshops and mentorship programs, making them accessible to individuals from diverse backgrounds, particularly those who may not typically engage with such practices. By demystifying the healing aspects of hairdressing, I hope to ignite curiosity and spark a desire for self-care within various communities, reinforcing that everyone deserves to experience the magic of self-transformation.

As I map out my goals for community impact, I am reminded of the profound connections I have formed with clients over the years. Each story shared in the salon chair has contributed to my understanding of the role hairdressing plays in self-expression and healing. Some clients come to me carrying heavy burdens, and through our conversations and the sacred exchange of energy during our sessions, we work together to uplift one another. I believe that the essence of these healing conversations can extend beyond the salon, creating a broader narrative surrounding beauty and wellness.

To amplify these narratives, I envision documenting the transformational stories of my clients and the families they inspire. By creating a visual platform, perhaps a blog or social media initiative I can spotlight their journeys of self-discovery and empowerment, thereby cultivating a deeper connection with those who may relate to their experiences. Sharing these stories will remind us that we are not alone in our struggles, and that the journey toward self-love is a communal one. I believe telling these narratives is crucial; it's a reminder that healing is a continual process, and it is often enriched by the stories of those who walked the path alongside us.

Another vital aspect of my vision for the future involves establishing a collective space for healing practitioners. I dream of creating a wellness center that brings together diverse healing modalities under one roof a sanctuary where individuals can explore various pathways to wellness. In this sanctuary, hairdressers, Reiki practitioners, massage therapists, and other holistic healers could collaborate to provide a curated experience that addresses the multifaceted needs of our clients. This ecosystem would foster a spirit of co-creation, allowing us to design workshops, events, and community outreach opportunities that elevate the importance of holistic well-being.

Through this center, we could host community events aimed at reducing stigma surrounding mental health and alternative healing practices. Organizing panel discussions, workshops, and seminars could create a dialogue, erasing the notions of skepticism that sometimes accompany new healing perspectives, and instead fostering a culture of openness and support. I believe in the power of education and connection to transcend preconceived notions about healing modalities. By inviting community members to be a part of these conversations, we can cultivate an environment where everyone feels empowered to take charge of their own healing journeys.

As I navigate through the vision for these future endeavors, I continue to check in with myself reflecting on the energy I wish to project and the intentions I want to manifest. I firmly believe that every step I take in this journey must be imbued with purpose and authenticity. As I attract opportunities to expand my practice, it's crucial to maintain a genuine connection with my core values, ensuring that my work remains steeped in love and compassion.

Looking ahead, I also see potential for collaborations with local artists. I envision art shows and showcases within the wellness space, where the work of local creatives can beautify our surroundings while inspiring conversations about healing and wellness. This integration of art, beauty, and healing would deepen the narrative of self-expression, inviting individuals to explore different avenues through which they can express themselves. The vibrancy of art combined with the transformative power of hairdressing would create an inspiring environment that encourages community members to tap into their creativity and celebrate their unique identities.

Amid story of these future aspirations lies an important commitment to sustainability. I recognize that the beauty industry often grapples with the consequences of environmental impact, which is why I aim to pioneer sustainable practices within my work. By sourcing Eco friendly products, minimizing waste in the salon, and educating clients on mindful consumption, I aspire to create an Eco-conscious approach to hairdressing that honors our planet. This commitment to sustainability can also trickle into the workshops and retreats I plan to offer, instilling an understanding of our interconnected essential with the Earth and the importance of nurturing and honoring our shared home.

As I cement my vision for the future, it is essential to remember that this journey is not solely about me; it's about the larger community we are building together. Every person who enters my salon or attends a workshop carries the potential for healing and transformation. I hold a deep hope that through my work, I can foster an environment where individuals can feel safe to explore, heal, and embrace their authentic selves. To me, this is the ultimate goal a future where hairdressing and healing not only coexist but thrive in harmony, celebrating the beauty of each person's unique journey.

This vision aligns seamlessly with my core belief that we are all interconnected. Every hair transformation, every Reiki session, and every shared story is a thread in the fabric of healing. I deeply hope to cultivate a sense of belonging among my clients and students while simultaneously nurturing the understanding that we each contribute to the collective healing of our communities. It is through this lens of unity that we can transcend individual limitations and empower one another.

As I conclude my reflections on the future of my practice, I feel a surge of anticipation for what lies ahead. The beauty of this journey is the infinite possibilities that await us. I embrace the challenges, knowing that growth often sprouts from discomfort. My intentions are clear, and my passion will fuel the collective healing I aspire to nurture. Together, we will continue this journey, weaving a tapestry of love, support, and healing that links hairdressing and holistic practices, one beautiful head at a time. The journey continues, and I am ready for whatever comes next.

Invitation to Readers

As I stand in my salon, weaving through the familiar scents of lavender and warm shea butter, I feel an overwhelming sense of gratitude. Each brush of my hand through a client's hair feels like a prayer not just for beauty, but for healing, love, connection, and empowerment. I look around and see the reflections of the countless souls who have graced my chair, shared their stories, and opened their hearts. They came seeking transformation, and in the alchemy of hair and healing, we discovered that change ripples far beyond the tangible. By fusing the deeply cultural art of African braiding with the universal energy of Reiki, Kadybeauty Seer offers a truly holistic beauty-healing experience: my clients leave not only with stunning hair, but with a clear energetic field and a renewed connection to their own inner truth.

This journey has been a tapestry woven with threads of trust, acceptance, and love. I feel compelled to reach out to you, dear reader, and invite you into this sacred experience. Wherever you are on your journey, whether you are standing on the precipice of change or gliding into new chapters, I encourage you to embrace the profound power of self-care, community, and healing as fundamental catalysts for your transformation.

Throughout this book, I've shared my own evolution, the journey of my craft, and the energies that intertwine hairdressing and Reiki healing. But it extends far beyond the confines of my story. Your path, though distinctly unique, is interwoven with the same universal truths that have shaped my experience. We are all inextricably linked; the energies we embody ripple outward, influencing those around us, just like the gentle waves in a calm pond. When we allow ourselves to heal, we create a pebble effect. Every act of self-love and healing you embrace has the power to send ripples of positivity into your community and beyond.

I invite you to pause and reflect upon your own life. What energies are you carrying? What stories do you tell yourself about your worth, your beauty, or your capacity for healing? Are you setting aside time to reconnect with your inner self, to engage in rituals that soothe your spirit? This is your moment to acknowledge your journey, the joys and the struggles. Every step you take toward nurturing yourself empowers not just you but the lives you touch each day. You have the agency to create needed changes and ripple outwards.

When I first stepped into the world of hairdressing, my ambitions were simple to create beauty. But over time, I learned that true beauty emanates from a deeper place, one anchored in self-acceptance and love. Each style I crafted mirrored not just a client's external appearance but their internal narratives, their triumphs, and their insecurities. Those moments have illuminated the truth that self-care is not merely a luxury; it is essential.

Self-care involves creating space to hear your own thoughts, dreams, and fears amidst the chaos of life. It's about learning to treat your soul with the same kindness and love that you would offer to a dear friend. As you consider your own self-care rituals, whether it's through meditation, journaling , or even a mindful cup of tea, ask yourself: How can you nurture your spirit today?

Community also forms the bedrock of our growth. As you practice self-care, reach out and extend your hand to others. The power of shared experience is transformative. When I began teaching workshops in my salon, I witnessed the incredible strength that arises when individuals gather with open hearts and shared intentions. Each participant brought their unique energies, creating a vibrant tapestry of hope and healing that empowered everyone involved.

Your community, be it your family, friends, or even fellow seekers holds immense potential for growth and healing. Together, you can create safe spaces for vulnerability, connection, and collective empowerment. I have seen how participants bond over shared challenges and deep-seated dreams, lifting each other as they embark on their individual journeys. You are not alone in this process; the shared experiences of others can guide you, support you, and uplift you during times of doubt.

As you contemplate your involvement in your community, consider how your unique gifts can contribute to the collective. How can you show up either as a healer, an encouragement , or a listener? Challenge yourself to step outside of your comfort zone, whether that means volunteering your time, sharing your talents, or simply listening to someone's story. Each act of kindness or vulnerability creates a ripple effect.

Also, remember the importance of healing. It is not a destination but a continuous journey. Healing occurs in layers, much like the intricate process of hairstyling, where each section of hair is carefully tended to, nourished, and shaped. As you embark on your own healing journey, know that it is okay to seek support when needed. Engage with professionals, healers, or a trusted friend who will hold space for you as you navigate through life's ups and downs. Trust that healing is a multi-faceted process; it' s not always linear, and that's perfectly alright.

I reflect on the multitude of clients who sat in my chair and bravely unveiled their stories to me stories of heartbreak, joy, disappointment, and triumph. Many expressed how hairstyling, coupled with the healing energy of Reiki, created space for them to release old wounds and embrace their authentic selves. This transformation unfolded in myriad forms, whether through a bold haircut or a joyous laughter shared during a treatment.

As you seek your transformation, think about the practitioners or guides who resonate with your spirit. Are there healers, mentors, or coaches whose energies align with your own? Allow yourself to be drawn to those who uplift and inspire you. Collective healing within our communities is further solidified through shared energies. It is in recognizing that we are all interconnected and that our experiences shape one another that we become open to expansive growth.

Let's take a moment to visualize your journey ahead. Imagine you've stepped into the life of your dreams, surrounded by vibrant energies and connections that uplift your spirit. Picture yourself confident in your own skin, radiating self-love and compassion. How will you get there? What are the actionable steps you can take today to embark on this journey further?

Consider crafting a vision board or journaling your dreams and intentions. Write down the steps you'll take to nurture your goals. These could be as simple as dedicating time to a new hobby, committing to a weekly self-care ritual, or even joining a community event to connect with others. Every small action will move you closer to the energetic alignment that you seek.

Embrace the bumps along the road. Each challenge transforms into an opportunity for growth, just as each client teaches me something new about hair, healing, or love. The resilience you cultivate through struggles will enable you to appreciate the joyful moments even more. With each lesson learned, you gather wisdom to share with others, fostering a rich legacy of healing within your community.

As I conclude this journey, I invite you to hold these thoughts close to your heart: You are worthy of love, healing, and transformation. Allow yourself to fully experience the richness of life, to dive into the depths of your soul, and to seek what truly sparks joy in your spirit. The world is waiting for your unique gifts, crafted through your journey.

Let this be the inception of your transformative adventure. Stand tall in your power, believe in your dreams, and let your light shine brightly. I am here to cheer you on, as your fellow traveler on this path. Let us embrace the journey together through healing, artistry, and connection and uplift one another in every step we take.

Through this invitation, I hope to ignite a fire within you. Your journey may not always be easy, but remember that you are equipped with the power of choice and intention to carve your unique path. Embrace each moment, celebrate every small victory, and never underestimate the significance of your presence in this world. You are destined for great transformations.

With love and encouragement, I invite you to embark on this adventure. The journey continues, and I can't wait to witness your story unfold.

Legacy of Healing

As Kadybeauty stood in her salon, the gentle hum of the world outside blended with the soft rustle of hair being styled and the warm laughter that often filled the space. It was a sanctuary not just for her clients but, most importantly, for herself. Each snip of the scissors was a rhythmic echo of her journey a journey that had nurtured not only her hands but her heart and spirit. In this contrast of beauty and vulnerability, Kady found a profound truth about her purpose: to leave a lasting legacy that went beyond the hair on her clients' heads, extending into their lives and the community around her.

Kady often reflected on the many chairs she had filled in her salon. Each client brought with them a story, an energy that crafted their unique narrative. It was in those tender moments of connection sharing dreams, struggles, and laughter that Kady discovered the essence of her work: empowerment. The transformations that occurred in her salon did not just manifest through hair; they traveled deep into the hearts and minds of those who sat in her chair. They were visible in the renewed sense of self-worth that shone in their eyes, in the confidence that radiated when they stepped out into the world.

This realization shaped Kady's vision for her legacy. She envisioned a ripple effect that would extend far beyond the salon's walls a legacy rooted in compassion and connection, where beauty and healing intertwined seamlessly. She wanted to nurture future generations, to instill the understanding that hairdressing was not only an art form but also a powerful medium for healing and self-discovery. Kady believed that hairstylists and healers alike have the unique ability to facilitate transformation, and she wanted to inspire others to recognize and embrace the potent energy that resides within their craft.

While hairdressing was her primary medium of expression, Kady understood the expansive nature of healing. She envisioned educating young hairdressers about the blend of beauty and energy work, where a simple haircut or style could become a transformative moment. She dreamed of holding workshops that emphasized this union, exploring techniques that incorporate mindfulness, meditation, and intention-setting into the hairstyling experience. Kady knew that when hairstylists, especially those who came from underrepresented communities, could harness their talents in ways that uplift and empower their clients, the impact would be transformational.

Kady's own journey was peppered with experiences that highlighted the need for compassion and understanding. As a young girl, she had often felt overshadowed by the societal norms surrounding beauty. The images portrayed in media often seemed unattainable, existing in a world that pushed her to conform rather than celebrate her rich cultural roots. These experiences fueled her desire to cultivate a salon environment that embraced diversity and authenticity, where every individual felt valued and acknowledged for who they truly were. It was vital for Kady to ensure that future generations of hairdressers recognized the importance of empowering their clients to embrace their uniqueness.

Empowerment was at the heart of Kady's vision, and it permeated every aspect of her work. In her internal musings, she often pondered how she could best serve her community, how to become a beacon of hope in their lives. To her, legacy was not about the accolades or recognition she might receive; it lived in the moments when a client looked in the mirror and saw not just a transformed exterior but the reflection of their inner strength. It was the joy of witnessing a young person leave the salon feeling like they could conquer the world, their confidence buoyed by the experience of change and kindness.

Kady also saw the opportunity to impact the broader community. She envisioned collaborating with local organizations focused on empowerment and healing. From hosting community events that fostered inclusivity to partnering with educational institutions to develop programs for aspiring hairdressers and healers, Kady felt a profound commitment to building bridges. In her mind, every effort was a way to create a network of support, where individuals uplift one another, tapping into a wellspring of creative and emotional potential.

One of the most profound aspects of Kady's legacy was the understanding that healing was a communal journey. While her work in the salon was deeply personal, it thrived in the connections she forged with her clients and the community. By nurturing relationships, she cultivated a culture of shared experiences and growth, where vulnerability was welcomed, and healing became a collective endeavor. Kady envisioned creating support groups that not only brought healing but also provided safe spaces for expression, where conversations could flourish and stories could be told and retold.

Throughout her reflections, Kady recognized the transformational power of storytelling. Each client who walked into her salon carried a wealth of experiences that shaped who they were. By encouraging them to share their stories, Kady opened up a channel for healing, inviting them to explore their journeys while seated in her chair. As she listened to their narratives, she often felt a spark of inspiration, reminding her that healing resided not just in words but in the profound exchange of energy that took place during these conversations.

Kady felt that it was essential to cultivate environments where these stories could flow freely. By weaving her own experiences in with those of her clients, she understood that they were co-authors of their narratives, co-creating paths toward self-discovery. She wanted to promote workshops that could harness this power, where clients would be guided in articulating their journeys through creative outlets such as writing, art, or even hairdressing techniques. These workshops would provide the tools for clients to narrate their transformations, empowering them and fostering a sense of ownership of their healing process.

Furthermore, Kady recognized the necessity of resilience within her legacy. There would inevitably be challenges, a truth she understood intimately. By embracing her vulnerabilities and acknowledging her own battles with self-acceptance, Kady became a strong advocate for mental health awareness. She spoke openly about her journey, believing it crucial to destigmatize conversations surrounding emotional struggles within the hairdressing community. Kady envisioned creating a mentorship program in which seasoned hairdressers could share their experiences to instill hope and resilience in younger professionals. Such initiatives would not only strengthen the community but foster an environment where future generations could navigate their own challenges with grace and support.

Empowered by her commitment to nurturing future generations, Kady's aspirations for her legacy were ambitious, yet deeply rooted in a sense of purpose. She often felt invigorated by the idea of creating a scholarship program for aspiring hairdressers from diverse backgrounds. By addressing the barriers many faced in pursuing their passion, she believed she could ignite a fire within countless young individuals who wished to make their mark in the world of beauty and healing. Kady envisioned inspiring them to embrace their cultural identities and experiences, reminding them that their stories were just as important as the ones told in magazines and on television.

Ultimately, Kady's legacy was about connection between herself and her clients, between her clients and each other, and within the community. She aspired to foster a culture where vulnerability was embraced, where everyone felt seen and appreciated. In her heart, she held a vision for a future brimming with compassion, where health and wellness became a collective mission instead of an individual endeavor.

In her solitude, Kady often meditated on the sacred nature of her work. While it sometimes felt overwhelming to carry the aspirations of future generations on her shoulders, she found solace in knowing that every step she took brought her closer to the fulfillment of her dreams. With gentle persistence, Kady learned to embrace the ebb and flow of her journey, trusting that every energetic exchange in her salon contributed to a greater legacy of healing.

As her thoughts drifted through her dreams and aspirations, Kady recognized that each day presented an opportunity to inspire. Whether through a simple smile, a heartfelt conversation, or an uplifting haircut that ignited confidence, Kady understood that her legacy was engraved in the hearts of those she touched. Her belief in the transformational power of hairdressing and healing led her to believe that true beauty transcended aesthetics; it resided in empowerment, connection, and the shared commitment to growth.

In this realization, Kady found the strength to embrace her role not only as a hairstylist but also as a teacher, mentor, and healer. With each passing day, she stepped into her purpose with renewed clarity, knowing that every moment in her salon was a thread being woven into the rich tapestry of her legacy one that celebrated healing, empowerment, and the undeniable connection between beauty and the spirit.

With deep gratitude for the path she had traveled, Kady envisioned the future an intricate network of empowered individuals carrying forward the lessons of compassion, guidance, and self-love. They would shape their destinies with courage and authenticity, forever acknowledging the sacred gift of healing that Kady so passionately fostered in her community.

As the sun dipped below the horizon and the salon transformed into a cozy haven, Kady's heart brimmed with excitement for the journey ahead. Her legacy was not merely a destination but an evolving rhythm of connection and growth, one that would resonate for generations to come. Kady was not just creating hairstyles; she was weaving a legacy filled with healing, empowerment, and love an alchemy of beauty that transcended the physical and touched the very essence of the human spirit.

Cheers to New Beginnings!

Thank you for joining me on this incredible journey! As we wrap up our exploration of hairdressing and Reiki, I hope you've felt the passion that pours out from every chapter a passion that I live and breathe every day. You've encountered the stories, the techniques, and the transformative power of our intertwined energies, and now it's your turn to weave your own magic into the world.

Remember, this book was designed not only to share my journey but also to spark inspiration within you. Embrace the new insights you've gained about energy alignment, community healing, and the art of self-care. Imagine how those elements can blend into your own life how you can become an artist of your existence, channeling your inner Kady to create magnificent change.

I can't stress enough how vital community is in this process. We grow, heal, and thrive together. So reach out, connect with the people around you, dive into your local communities, and remember that healing isn't a solitary experience it's a vibrant tapestry woven from our collective journeys.

As you step out of these pages and into your world, think of the practical exercises, meditations, and the nuggets of wisdom I offered. Use them as tools in your toolkit; let them guide you in your beautiful alchemy toward a life filled with meaning, joy, and transformation. Trust in yourself, and don't be afraid to connect deeper with your own energy.

I genuinely hope this book has been as empowering for you to read as it was for me to write. Your journey doesn't end here; this is just the beginning. Keep tuning into that energy, keep exploring, and may the magic of hairdressing and healing continue to unfold in your life. I can't wait to hear about your transformations; let's keep this dialogue going! You are amazing, and the world needs your light!

With endless gratitude, Kadybeauty Seer the Sword of Truth.

Khadijatou

About the Author

Khadijatou, known as Kadybeauty, is a holistic hairdresser, Reiki healer, and spiritual guide whose salon is more than a beauty destination — it's a sacred space for transformation. Born in Senegal and spiritually awakened through her life journey across Africa, Europe, and the U.S., she has fused ancestral hair rituals with modern healing practices. As a seer and intuitive, Kady weaves energy work, Ruqyah, and deep intention into every braid and cut, helping clients reconnect with their inner divinity. Her signature styles reflect more than beauty; they radiate purpose, faith, and truth. Through her work and writing, she invites readers to embrace self-love, spiritual alignment, and divine identity.

https://kadybeauty.us

https://www.facebook.com/share/1EbTPToU2J/?mibextid=wwXIfr

https://www.facebook.com/share/16R6WsNs96/?mibextid=wwXIfr

Also by Khadijatou Ndoye

A sacred journey of hair, healing, and heritage. Kadybeauty Seer weaves her story as a holistic hairdresser and Reiki healer into a tapestry of ancestral wisdom, divine rituals, and transformative beauty. This book is both a mirror and a map—for those ready to crown themselves in truth.

Book Title: Kadybeauty Seer: The Alchemy of Hair and Healing. This poetic, soul-stirring book explores the alchemy of African hair braiding and Reiki healing. Khadijatou "Kadybeauty Seer" Ndoye shares her sacred path from Senegal to the international salon, offering wisdom, rituals, and affirmations to guide you back to your divine crown.

www.ingramcontent.com/pod-product-compliance
Lightning Source LLC
Chambersburg PA
CBHW070619130626
46556CB00001B/413